POLICING MENTAL HEALTH, VULNERABILITY AND RISK

POLICING MENTAL HEALTH, VULNERABILITY AND RISK

THE PROFESSIONAL POLICING CURRICULUM IN PRACTICE

BRIAN WILLIAMS

SERIES EDITOR: TONY BLOCKLEY

Routledge
Taylor & Francis Group
LONDON AND NEW YORK

First published in 2023 by Critical Publishing Ltd

Published 2025 by Routledge
4 Park Square, Milton Park, Abingdon, Oxon OX14 4RN
605 Third Avenue, New York, NY 10017

Routledge is an imprint of the Taylor & Francis Group, an informa business

British Library Cataloguing in Publication Data
A CIP record for this book is available from the British Library

ISBN: 9781041056447 (hbk)
ISBN: 9781915080561 (pbk)
ISBN: 9781041056454 (ebk)

Cover and text design by Out of House Limited

DOI: 10.4324/9781041056454

CONTENTS

ABOUT THE SERIES EDITOR

TONY BLOCKLEY

Tony Blockley is Head of School, Criminology, Investigation and Policing at Leeds Trinity University, responsible for coordinating policing higher education, including developing programmes and enhancing the current provision in line with the Police Education Qualification Framework (PEQF) and supporting the College of Policing. He served within policing for over 30 years, including a role as Chief Superintendent and Head of Crime.

ABOUT THE AUTHOR

BRIAN WILLIAMS

Brian Williams is the learning skills lead and a lecturer in policing at Lincoln College on the professional policing degree. He spent 30 years working within the Metropolitan and Lincolnshire Police, gaining considerable experience in a wide variety of policing roles and ended his policing career as a Sergeant. Following retirement, he led a training team within Lincolnshire Police in partnership with G4S as the policing skills manager with responsibility for training student police officers. At Lincoln College he teaches across further and higher education, and is an advocate for professional practice underpinned by academic theory.

FOREWORD

Police professionalism has seen significant developments over recent years, including the implementation of the Vision 2025 and the establishment of the Police Education Qualification Framework (PEQF). There is no doubt that policing has become complex, and that complexity and associated challenges increase day by day with greater scrutiny, expectation and accountability. The educational component of police training and development therefore allows officers to gain a greater understanding and appreciation of the theories and activities associated with high quality policing provision.

The scholastic element of the Vision 2025 provides an opportunity to engage in meaningful insight and debate around some of the most sensitive areas of policing while also taking the lessons of the past and utilising them to develop the service for the future. While there are many books and articles on numerous subjects associated with policing, this new series – *The Professional Policing Curriculum in Practice* – provides an insightful opportunity to start that journey. It distils the key concepts and topics within policing into an accessible format, combining theory and practice to provide you with a secure basis of knowledge and understanding.

With policing now a degree-level entry profession, this has provided a unique opportunity to develop fully up-to-date books for student and trainee police officers that focus on the content of the PEQF curriculum, are tailored specifically to the new pre-join routes, and reflect the diversity and complexity of twenty-first-century society. Each book is standalone, but they also work together to layer information as you progress through your programme. The pedagogical features of the books have been carefully designed to improve your understanding and critical thinking skills within the context of policing. They include learning objectives, case studies, evidence-based practice examples, critical thinking and reflective activities, and summaries of key concepts. Each chapter also includes a guide to further reading, meaning you do not have to spend hours researching to find that piece of information you are looking for.

This book examines some of the most critical elements of policing; how policing recognises and responds to incidents of vulnerability and, importantly, how it engages in a proactive position, learning from the lessons of the past to anticipate and so create opportunities to prevent crimes within this area in the future. The book also seeks to explore and understand the challenges of victims and the drivers of the perpetrators in order to provide greater knowledge and appreciation of the key factors. The range of case studies enables you to explore these critical areas and reflect on future practices, while all the content is intended to promote enquiry and encourage additional reading and research.

Having been involved in policing for over 40 years, the benefits of these books are obvious to me: I see them becoming the go-to guides for the PEQF curriculum across all the various programmes associated with the framework, while also having relevance for more experienced officers.

Tony Blockley
Discipline Head: Policing
Leeds Trinity University

CHAPTER 1
THE COMPLEXITIES OF POLICING VULNERABLE PERSONS IN SOCIETY

LEARNING OBJECTIVES

AFTER READING THIS CHAPTER YOU WILL BE ABLE TO:

- **explain the definition of vulnerability utilised within policing;**
- **discuss the different interpretations of vulnerability;**
- **understand the reasons why vulnerability is such a complex issue for policing.**

INTRODUCTION

The current definition of vulnerability has been created and agreed by the College of Policing, the National Police Chiefs' Council (an organisation which represents all the Chief Constables) (NPCC, nd) and all Home Office police services. The concept of vulnerability is one which has gained considerable traction within policing in the last 20 years. Previously, policing cannot be said to have been particularly sympathetic, certainly as a collective organisation towards vulnerability. Vulnerable victims and witnesses were often left largely to fend for themselves prior to the Youth Justice and Criminal Evidence Act (YJCEA) 1999, which introduced the concept of special measures to provide a degree of support and protection to vulnerable victims and witnesses. Vulnerable members of communities were also often neglected by the police and other agencies; it was after the deaths of Fiona Pilkington and her daughter Francesca Hardwick in 2007, who had suffered ten years of abuse from local youths aimed at the daughter's severe disabilities, that policing and other agencies again looked at their responsibilities towards vulnerable members of society.

As this book determines, vulnerability can be related to a vast variety of factors. This chapter helps you to focus on the key policing definition of vulnerability and to develop a real understanding of different agency definitions. The definitions underpin the need for a consistent and professional approach to dealing with people at risk of harm as a result of their vulnerability. Finally, it considers why policing vulnerability is such a complex issue.

CRITICAL THINKING ACTIVITY 1.1

LEVEL 4

Consider what you know about society and the individuals that make up local communities.

- How would you define vulnerability in a general sense to include those who are at more risk of harm than others?

Sample answers are provided at the end of this book.

HOW DO THE POLICE DEFINE VULNERABILITY?

The College of Policing first started to use the THRIVE definition of vulnerability in 2021 (THRIVE is a mnemonic which is used to assess certain factors which determine the threat, harm, risk, investigation, vulnerability and engagement). The definition states:

> *a person is vulnerable if, as a result of their situation or circumstances, they are unable to take care of or protect themselves or others from harm or exploitation.*
>
> (College of Policing, 2021a)

Hopefully you feel a sense of agreement with these words. There may even be a feeling of unease knowing that policing has previously not always been so empathetically minded. The definition is extremely flexible and allows for individual circumstances and situations to be considered. It demands that the risk of harm be part of the equation. Chapter 3 examines the intrinsic and extrinsic factors which you need to be mindful of as part of this equation. It raises issues such as the impact of early life experiences, mental illness, age and learning disabilities, to name four intrinsic factors. It also considers some extrinsic factors, such as the environment the person is in, the situation in which the person finds themselves and the presence of an offender. While policing cannot solve all the problems in society on its own, it needs to take responsibility for its own actions and protect the vulnerable from harm or risk of harm.

WHAT IS HARM OR RISK OF HARM?

The police, of course, are not the only agency that needs to be mindful around working with individuals who are vulnerable and at increased risk of harm.

Before discussing how partner agencies view vulnerability it is important to define harm as a concept. Harm is either '*physical or mental damage*' or injury, and '*mischief or hurt*' (www.merriam-webster.com/dictionary/harm).

It is not quite as simple as having a brief definition of the concept of harm. Criminologists have developed a theory of the '*social harm approach*' from historical perspectives of harm being caused both in a criminal context but also in a social context. Pemberton (2016) discussed how the social harm approach identified the narrow definition of crime where it focuses on certain crimes at the expense of others. So, murders, rapes and serious assaults are prioritised due to the seriousness of the harm experienced and given a keen focus as crimes to be solved, as opposed to other crimes which, although there may be many more victims – for example, thefts, damage and minor assaults – are effectively downgraded. While the idea of the social harm approach now extends beyond the borders of criminology, it does raise an interesting comparable consideration in terms of how the police have traditionally dealt with crimes and anti-social behaviour involving vulnerable people. Is there a symmetry between narrow crimes and the wider concept of social harm, and a crime involving a non-vulnerable person and one involving a vulnerable person? If police have traditionally adopted a narrow focus around victim types, as in recent child sexual exploitation in Rochdale and Rotherham, or in the manner of investigations into reports of abuse against infants such as Baby P and Victoria Climbié, then this could explain the apparent reluctance to consider the issue of vulnerability and risk.

The enthusiastic motivation of the police in the second decade of the twenty-first century is displayed through one role of policing being clearly defined as:

> *Reducing crime and protecting the vulnerable are core priorities for the police service.*
>
> (NPCC, 2016)

There is a need to explore the circumstances that could make an individual vulnerable and therefore render them more likely at risk of harm and potentially becoming a victim of crime.

CRITICAL THINKING ACTIVITY 1.2

LEVEL 4

- List five situations or circumstances that could render a person vulnerable to the risk of harm.

Sample answers are provided at the end of this book.

This book examines numerous policing themes where victims could be vulnerable. Examples of such themes include modern slavery, county lines gangs, child sexual exploitation and online abuse and bullying. Factors such as mental illness and domestic abuse can also render an individual susceptible to increased risk of harm. What can be stated categorically, however, is that there are certain individuals who will be attractive to the criminal fraternity and abusers, and many, if not all, the circumstances considered above will be present.

WHO IS VULNERABLE?

Many people in society could be thought of as vulnerable. Vulnerability may be temporary or permanent, a person with a mental disorder, a person with an impairment of intelligence or social functioning, a young person, an elderly person or a person in a particular place during certain circumstances. But is every such person vulnerable per se? This is a good question, and it is important that we spend some time examining how a variety of agencies that work with the police would define vulnerability.

Public Health England uses the following definition:

> *Being vulnerable is defined as in need of special care, support, or protection because of age, disability, risk of abuse or neglect.*
>
> (GOV.UK, 2022a)

Another important consideration is the differentiation between adult and child vulnerability. The National Health Service (NHS) defines vulnerable adults as

> *any adult (person over the age of 18) unable to take care of themselves or protect themselves from exploitation. Many factors can influence adult vulnerability, experiences of vulnerability in childhood may negatively impact adults in later life – particularly if someone has fewer protective factors in place, such as a supportive family or a stable household income.*
>
> (GOV.UK, 2022a)

If you compare this to the earlier policing definition you should identify many similarities. These include a consideration of the situation and circumstances a person may find themselves in and their inability to take care of or look after themselves.

HOW DOES A CHILD DIFFER FROM AN ADULT WHEN CONSIDERING VULNERABILITY?

In terms of child vulnerability, the Office for Health Improvement and Disparities claims that

- the individual characteristics of a child, or,
- the fact that the child can suffer as a result of an action or inaction by another person, or,
- the physical and social environment of the child,

can all increase the risk of and create vulnerability for the child, which make poor outcomes more likely (GOV.UK, 2022a).

Following the Covid-19 pandemic and government safety measures, children were at an enhanced risk of harm due to the closing of educational establishments. This meant that one of the main ways for children to report harm was removed. It also meant that a natural place of safety was also unavailable to them. In 2020, a former Children's Commissioner, Anne Longfield, highlighted concerns that '*Children fall through the gaps*' (Henshaw, 2021).

She was concerned that child victims at risk of harm through a multitude of factors could become invisible and therefore beyond the reach of supportive agencies.

In an earlier report, on behalf of the office of the Children's Commissioner, nine domains of child vulnerability were identified.

Table 1.1 Domains of child vulnerability (adapted from Children's Commissioner, 2017)

1	Safeguarding concerns or in local authority care.
2	Health or disability.
3	Economic circumstances.
4	Family circumstances or characteristics.
5	Educational engagement.
6	Involvement in offending and/or anti-social behaviour.
7	Experience of abuse/exploitation.
8	Missing or absent children.
9	Membership of a minority population.

Many of these '*domains*' feature in considerations around early life events or adverse childhood experiences. This series of factors and the implications for the children who experience them will be a golden thread throughout this book. It is also acknowledged by the Children's Commissioner that while membership of a vulnerable group can lead to '*poorer outcomes*', it does not automatically mean that they will receive poorer outcomes. This point by the Children's Commissioner is an indication of how complex this area is.

What this brief review of legislation and agency considerations clarifies is that the very nature of vulnerability is difficult to define in line with the varied needs and responsibilities of different agencies. This difficulty of consistent and comparable definitions of vulnerability is borne out of agencies having slightly different aims and objectives. Another key factor which cannot be dismissed arose because of government austerity measures from 2010 onwards. Post 2010, agencies, while recognising that society had far more vulnerable individuals in it than ever previously considered, suddenly had fewer resources to address the situations that were being identified.

The College of Policing recognised that:

> *Vulnerability-related demand has increased for the police service, and a proportionate and effective response is required to manage it.*
>
> (College of Policing, 2021a)

LEGISLATION AND VULNERABILITY

There are several pieces of legislation which impact on our considerations here. A key one is found in the Care Act 2014.

THE CARE ACT 2014

An important aspect of the Care Act is that the word vulnerable should no longer be used, being replaced by adult safeguarding. This change in phraseology is recommended for all partners. This raises an interesting question around how an adult may be at risk of requiring safeguarding.

> *An adult at risk of abuse or neglect is defined as someone who has needs for care and support, who is experiencing, or at risk of abuse or neglect and as a result of their care needs is unable to protect themselves.*
>
> (Care Act 2014, section 42)

THE HOUSING ACT 1996

Another notable piece of legislation is the Housing Act 1996. This legislation considers the impact of repeat victimisation and anti-social behaviour on a vulnerable person (section 218A). In section 189 (1) consideration is given to a person who is vulnerable as a result of old age, mental illness, handicap or physical disability or other special reason. This consideration of vulnerability is also reflected in the context of the Homelessness Reduction Act 2017.

THE CHILDREN ACT 1989 AND 2004

In terms of child vulnerability, the legislative context commences with the Children Act 1989. One of the central pillars of the act is that the welfare of the child is absolutely and totally incontrovertible. While this piece of legislation is wide and encompassing the protection of children per se, it does provide an indication as to where a child may be '*vulnerable*', although it does not provide any legal classifications or definitions. Section 17 (10) discusses a child who is in need. The first consideration is around achieving and maintaining '*a reasonable standard of health and development*'. This health and development can be '*significantly impaired*' or '*likely to be impaired*' without support under this legislation, or, as this subsection goes on to state, if the child is disabled. The interpretation of what is a reasonable standard of development is quite wide and considers physical development, educational development and emotional development, to name but three in section 17 (11).

The legislative support around safeguarding children and intervening when it is both necessary and in the interests of the child was enhanced through the Children Act 2004. This legislation was borne out of the poor practices that were found in child abuse cases such as that of Victoria Climbié.

THE MENTAL CAPACITY ACT 2005

A final piece of legislation to consider in the context of vulnerability is the Mental Capacity Act 2005. There is considerable debate around the policing of mental illness and has been for some time. Due to the austerity process and withdrawal of funding from frontline services such as those that support individuals with mental illness, much activity relating to mental disorder has been diverted to the attention of the police. The police had restricted powers from the Mental Health Act 1983, mainly around the use of section 136, whereby the police could remove any individual apparently suffering from a mental disorder from a public place to a place of safety. Due to the funding crisis in mental health services, there were fewer places of safety which were suitable for individuals suffering from mental illness. The police, as the last line of defence within society, when forced to intervene were left with the only viable place of safety, a police cell. This meant that individuals with mental illness were often criminalised as a result of police interventions or held in less-than-ideal surroundings for up to 72 hours while mental health assessments were conducted. As part of a change in direction around dealing with individuals with mental impairment, the Mental Capacity Act was enacted in 2005.

> *Police officers may need to make immediate decisions that relate to containing, controlling and potentially restraining an individual who lacks the capacity to make the decision in question for themself, while awaiting further input or direction from a health or social care professional.*
>
> (College of Policing, 2016a)

While the Mental Capacity Act (MCA) does not abdicate responsibility for the police, it does change the landscape around dealing with such individuals and it also reinforces the needs of other, more appropriate agencies to take responsibility for these individuals. The College of Policing provides guidance and direction to officers interpreting this legislation. They suggest situations such as persons attempting or threatening suicide or seriously injured but refusing medical treatment are among those where officers could utilise the MCA legislation.

Table 1.2 Definitions of vulnerability: a comparison

	Definition
Police	*[A] person is vulnerable if, as a result of their situation or circumstances, they are unable to take care of or protect themselves or others from harm or exploitation.* (College of Policing, 2021a)
Office for National Statistics	*Being vulnerable is defined as in need of special care, support, or protection because of age, disability, risk of abuse or neglect.* (ONS, 2021)
National Health Service	*Aged 18 years or over; who may be in need of community care services by reason of mental or other disability, age or illness; and who is or may be unable to take care of him or herself, or unable to protect him or herself against significant harm or exploitation.* (GOV.UK, 2022a)
Care Act 2014	*An adult at risk of abuse or neglect is defined as someone who has needs for care and support, who is experiencing, or is at risk of, abuse or neglect, and as a result of their care needs is unable to protect themselves.* (Care Act 2014, section 42)
Public Health England	*'[V]ulnerable children' are defined as any children at greater risk of experiencing physical or emotional harm and/or experiencing poor outcomes because of one or more factors in their lives.* (Public Health England, 2020)
Main comparable points – all definitions	• *Situation and circumstances – personal factors, environmental factors* • *Unable to take care of self (or others)* • *Likelihood of risk of harm (or exploitation, neglect)*

Finally, in terms of legal procedure it is important to mention two other processes. Firstly, the advent of special measures for vulnerable and intimidated victims and witnesses, which arrived with the advent of the Youth Justice and Criminal Evidence Act 1999. The Crown Prosecution Service describes special measures as:

> *... a series of provisions that help vulnerable and intimidated witnesses give their best evidence in court and help to relieve some of the stress associated with giving evidence. Special measures apply to prosecution and defence witnesses, but not to the defendant and are subject to the discretion of the court.*
>
> (CPS, 2021a)

Table 1.3 Vulnerability definition (adapted from the Youth Justice and Criminal Evidence Act 1999)

Definition of vulnerability: section 16 Youth Justice and Criminal Evidence Act 1999	
All witnesses under the age of 18 (child witnesses) Witnesses whose '*quality of evidence*' is likely to be diminished due to the witness: • suffering from a mental disorder; • having a significant impairment of intelligence and social functioning; • having a physical disability; • suffering from a physical disorder.	
Comparison with other definitions of vulnerability	• *Situation and circumstances – personal factors* • *Likely to be unable to take care of self* • *Likelihood of risk of harm (if not supported by Special Measures)*

While the provision of special measures can be seen as a positive step in recognising and safeguarding vulnerable victims and witnesses, they are still dependent upon agreement from the criminal justice system to be applied.

The second development which has assisted vulnerable victims receiving a fair and appropriate service from the police can be seen in the Victims' Code of Practice. The most recent code was introduced in 2021 to replace an earlier code from 2005. The Victims' Code provides a series of minimum standards (rights) that a victim of crime can expect to receive from the '*relevant*' service providers. Right 4 is to be referred to victim support services and to have those services cater for their specific individual needs. The Victims' Code discusses vulnerability here as in certain circumstances the victim is entitled to Enhanced Rights.

Table 1.4 Definition of vulnerability within the Victims' Code

Enhanced rights: Victims' Code You are eligible for Enhanced Rights under this code as a vulnerable victim if: • you are under the age of 18 at the time of the offence; or • the quality of your evidence is likely to be affected because: – you suffer from mental disorder; – you have a significant impairment of intelligence and social functioning; – you have a physical disability; – you suffer from a physical disorder.

The Victims' Code is another example of how the criminal justice system recognises vulnerability and provides support for individuals as a result. It is highly recommended that you visit https://assets.publishing.service.gov.uk/government/uploads/system/uploads/attachment_data/file/974376/victims-code-2020.pdf and consider the code in the context of vulnerability.

EVIDENCE-BASED POLICING

The College of Policing lead on the response of the police and in 2021 stated:

> *We have adopted the THRIVE (threat, harm, risk, investigation, vulnerability and engagement) definition of vulnerability.*
>
> (College of Policing, 2021a)

The overarching ambition of this approach is to allow policing to have a professional and consistent approach to dealing with incidents and crimes being reported. The first requirement for the police is to identify any vulnerabilities that an individual making a report or subject of a report may have. The police then consider the vulnerabilities in the context of whether they create harm or the risk of harm in the circumstances. If there is the possibility of harm or the risk of harm, then the police conduct an assessment. This then will provide the police with a risk-assessed approach which allows them to take any appropriate action or gain the support and involvement of a partner agency.

The THRIVE approach may appear contradictory to a new officer at first. Two identical incidents involving anti-social behaviour, but with different victims, could see the incident with a vulnerable victim receiving a prompt and proactive response by police linking in with a partner agency to support the victim, whereas the incident with a victim deemed not vulnerable may be resolved in a less proactive way, possibly by being referred to a partner agency with no actual police involvement. This differentiated approach demonstrates the risk-assessed decision-making process that is undertaken by police officers and call handlers when dealing with such reports.

REFLECTIVE PRACTICE 1.1

LEVEL 5

As a new police officer, the national decision model (NDM) (College of Policing, 2013a) will be used to assist you with making decisions such as those that require a THRIVE approach. The NDM is in essence a structured process to making a decision, allowing

→

you to provide a rationale as to why you follow a certain course of action, or indeed why you may not. Research the six stages of the NDM at www.college.police.uk/app/national-decision-model/national-decision-model and consider the importance of the Code of Ethics and Professional Standards in the context of a THRIVE approach.

- Does reliance on the Code of Ethics ensure that THRIVE decisions will be made correctly?

Sample answers are provided at the end of this book.

POLICING SPOTLIGHT

In 2009 the final report of the Independent Police Complaints Commission (IPCC) into the deaths of Fiona Pilkington and her daughter Francesca was published. The well-documented failings of Leicestershire Police and other agencies laid bare how policing in particular approached matters and allegations relating to anti-social behaviour, harassment and minor criminality in relation to circumstances where vulnerability was a central factor. Recommendation 3 of the final report states:

> *Leicestershire Constabulary's definition of a vulnerable person needs to reflect a person's circumstances as well as them as an individual. Failure to do this could result in persons in a similar situation to Fiona Pilkington being considered in isolation and not treated as vulnerable.*
>
> (IPCC, 2009)

The police did not consider the complainant, Fiona Pilkington, to be vulnerable, even though she was making allegations in relation to her vulnerable daughter. This led to the family not being identified as a '*vulnerable family unit*', which in turn led to the police not taking the matters reported very seriously. The IPCC does make the observation in its conclusions that, even allowing for the non-identification of the vulnerability issue, Fiona was reporting anti-social behaviour and harassment but did not receive the level of service that should be expected in those circumstances.

What was lacking in the Fiona Pilkington case was a recognised definition of vulnerability and a system such as THRIVE to risk assess each incident and allegation. This in essence is an illustration of how complex it is for policing to evaluate matters involving vulnerable people alongside the reality of harm or the risk of harm.

It can be accepted that the College of Policing definition of vulnerability is now a collective working definition within policing. It is also clear that many of the partner agencies that work alongside the police have also determined their own definitions, and that the definitions have considerable similarities. The key question at this point is why is it important for the police and partner agencies such as social services and health services to be working to similar definitions? The answer to the question is simple but also illustrates the complexities of the concept. Each agency will need its own definition of vulnerability to meet its organisational aims, so the NHS will need a definition which ensures their duty of care is met to its patients. Likewise, social services will need to determine a definition for adults and one for children to ensure their focus is supportive towards individual needs. The police have perhaps the most difficult task of all, not because investigating crime is incredibly problematic but rather because they have become the service of last resort for so many vulnerable people who have not actually been a victim of crime. While many see this as '*a waste of police time*', it is crucial to see police intervention as a positive interaction with a vulnerable individual which, if handled well, could be an intervening factor to prevent the vulnerable individual falling victim to future harm.

While the Pilkington report was a significant statement into police failings, it did not prove to be the '*watershed*' moment in ensuring vulnerability was properly assessed and appropriate support measures made available, as some of these failings were replicated in the case of Bijan Ebrahimi in 2013.

WHY IS POLICING VULNERABLE PERSONS SUCH A COMPLEX ISSUE?

This book examines the intrinsic and extrinsic factors that have a bearing on an individual's vulnerability, whether temporary or permanent (see Chapter 3), factors such as mental disorders and other forms of impairment. This is further compounded by the consideration of how someone becomes a victim, and theories of victimology will add to the mix. Another complex factor is the range of criminal groups who seek vulnerable victims as part of their criminal aspirations, such as modern slavery, county lines gangs and child exploitation, child sexual exploitation and online bullying. Another area of policing where complexity creates barriers for vulnerable victims is that of domestic abuse. A very simple view of crime is that an offender identifies or locates a victim, and a crime occurs. This may be the timeline of many crimes and leads to the creation of many victims. The complexity, however, is when consideration is made as to what additional factors can cause an individual to become a victim. As this chapter has intimated, individuals with vulnerabilities can become victims because of:

- personal factors;
- environmental factors;
- situational factors.

Consider a 15 year-old child who decides to run away from home. Due to age (personal factors) the individual is vulnerable and a viable target for county lines gangs. Approached and groomed by the criminal group (situational factors), the youngster is soon drawn into the murky world of drugs supply, and transported into a market town elsewhere in the country (environmental factors). This child is at risk of vanishing, away from their natural environment, family, school and friends. A vulnerability exploited by criminals, and one where the challenge to the police is perhaps one of intimidation by the criminals which prevents the youngster from reaching out.

SUMMARY OF KEY CONCEPTS

Establishing a viable working definition of vulnerability which can be easily understood and identified by all agencies had proved to be a struggle for a considerable time. Despite high-profile failures of safeguarding individuals – Fiona Pilkington and her daughter, the child victims of sexual abuse in Rotherham, victims of modern slavery, online abuse and county lines – it has taken a long time to find a viable definition. The content of this chapter helps you to:

- identify a policing definition of vulnerability;
- understand why partner agencies of the police may have slightly different definitions of vulnerability, but be able to evaluate comparable factors in such definitions;
- explain the term '*harm*' and the concept of the risk of harm;
- recognise legislation and other legal processes that have been created to support vulnerable individuals.

CHECK YOUR KNOWLEDGE

1. What does the acronym THRIVE stand for?

2. What is harm?

3. What similarities are there between definitions of vulnerability within policing, the NHS and social services?

4. What does the Victims' Code provide for vulnerable victims?

5. Identify three special measures which could be suitable for a vulnerable victim required to give evidence in a court case.

Sample answers are provided at the end of this book.

FURTHER READING

The College of Policing web pages covering vulnerability and risk are a searchable resource around identifying vulnerability and related risk guidelines. www.college.police.uk/guidance/vulnerability-related-risks/introduction-vulnerability-related-risk

CHAPTER 2
THE KEY DRIVERS FOR THE POLICE RESPONSE TO ISSUES OF VULNERABILITY

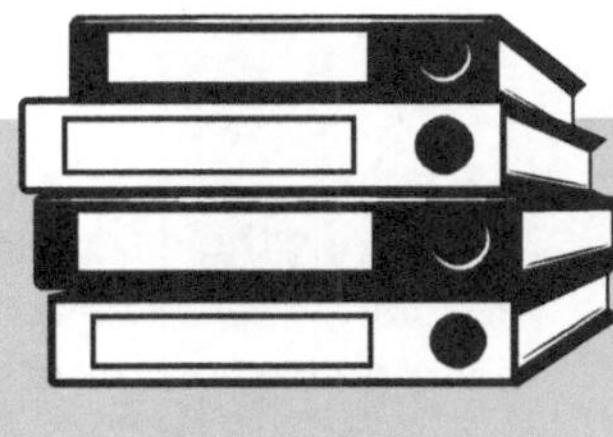

LEARNING OBJECTIVES

AFTER READING THIS CHAPTER YOU WILL BE ABLE TO:

- **discuss the impact of police failures leading up to the PEEL report into Police Effectiveness 2015 (Vulnerability);**
- **explain key drivers for an improved police response to issues of vulnerability;**
- **explain the principle of professional curiosity and discuss how it links into '*ethical*' policing;**
- **examine the concept of risk in relation to policing vulnerable individuals;**
- **explain the reasons for an increased demand for police services arising from the reporting of child sex abuse.**

INTRODUCTION

The previous chapter introduced you to the concept and definition of vulnerability. It explored how the police have historically dealt with vulnerable people and the subsequent evolvement of the THRIVE definition of vulnerability used in the police from 2021, which illustrated how the police dealt with issues of vulnerability before that point. This chapter provides a timeline of the key drivers, including lessons learnt from inquiries and investigations as well as legislative changes. It also considers the concept of risk which will add to the knowledge around the concept of harm in Chapter 1, particularly as the nuanced approach is now to identify the risk of harm to an individual with the THRIVE framework as a structure to follow. It looks at the concept of professional curiosity, a personal approach and skill demanded of all police officers when dealing with incidents. Professional curiosity involves '*thinking outside the box*' and asking relevant questions to gather historical and current information. Finally, it considers, through the use of case studies, reasons why the reporting of sex abuse against children rose rapidly, resulting in an increased demand on police resources.

CRITICAL THINKING ACTIVITY 2.1

LEVEL 5

- Considering the discussion around vulnerability in the previous chapter, research and identify five occasions where the police have struggled to deal with vulnerability appropriately in the last 25 years. Record your observations and set out why you think there was room for improvement in the police response.

Sample answers are provided at the end of this book.

The research you conducted may have been driven by a knowledge of certain events from the last 25 years when you were aware that the police and other partner agencies did not deal with situations particularly well. There are a number of case studies below, many of which are considered in this book, which you may have listed.

- The death of Victoria Climbié in 2000 – tortured and murdered by her great-aunt and her partner.
- The child sexual exploitation (CSE) scandal in Rochdale – allegations of child sexual abuse between 2008–09.
- The CSE scandal in Rotherham – allegations of CSE between 1997–2013.
- The death of Fiona Pilkington and her daughter Francesca in 2007. Following ten years of bullying and anti-social behaviour, the mother killed herself and her daughter.
- The death of Baby P – the murder of Peter Connelly by his mother and her partner.
- The death of Stephen Lawrence in 1999. Racist murder in South London.
- The murder of Breck Bednar in 2014. Murdered by Lewis Daynes following the online grooming of Breck.
- The murder of Holly Gazzard in 2014. Murdered by an estranged boyfriend who had been stalking her.
- The murder of Daniel Pelka in 2012. Murdered by his mother and her partner.
- The murder of Alice Ruggles in 2012. Murdered by her estranged boyfriend who had been stalking her.
- The murder of Angela Wrightson in 2014. Murdered by two teenage girls.

Each of the tragedies listed were not simply a tragic incident. Many, if not most, were avoidable, but all featured an element of vulnerability. All also had an element of the risk of harm present, but none were afforded sufficient protection to prevent the harm that eventually befell the victims.

The failings of several authorities in the last 20 years are illustrated in Table 2.1 through a series of reviews, inquiry reports and serious case reviews.

Table 2.1 Policing vulnerability: key drivers for change

Year	Key driver for change	Comments
2003	Lord Laming inquiry report	Report following inquiry into the death of Victoria Climbié.
2008	Serious Case Review into the death of Baby P	Findings of the Serious Case Review into the death of Peter Connelly (Baby P).
2009	IPCC report death of Fiona Pilkington	The Independent Police Complaints Commission (IPCC) report into the failings of Leicestershire police and its partners following the deaths of Fiona Pilkington and her daughter, Francesca.
2011	Achieving Best Evidence	Introduction of the *Achieving Best Evidence* manual to improve investigations involving vulnerable interviewees.
2013	Serious Case Review – child sexual exploitation – Rochdale	Independent inquiry report into the failings of Greater Manchester Police and its partners in relation to child sexual exploitation in Rochdale.
2014	The Jay report	Independent inquiry report into the failings of South Yorkshire Police and its partners in relation to child sexual exploitation in Rotherham.
2015	PEEL report – police effectiveness (Vulnerability)	Report by His Majesty's Inspectorate of Constabulary (HMIC) into how the police identify, protect and support individuals with vulnerability.
2016	National Crime Prevention Strategy	A strategic review of how crime is investigated with reduced victimisation being one of the main outcomes to tackle vulnerabilities associated with victimisation.
2016	*Policing Vision 2025*	A transformation document for policing looking forward ten years where better integration with partners will improve outcomes for citizens and protect the vulnerable.
2020	National Vulnerability Action Plan 2020–22	A two-year action plan devised by the National Police Chiefs' Council (NPCC) to address areas of weakness in the policing response.
2021	College of Policing definition of vulnerability	A new definition to spot signs of vulnerability, create an environment where risk can be identified and harm avoided, and individuals kept safe.
2021	Victims' Code of Practice	A revised version of a code of practice for victims of crime.

The following three key drivers highlight how policing reacted to the many serious case reviews, public inquiry reports, IPCC and Independent Office for Police Conduct (IOPC) investigation reports, recommendations and lessons learnt. Those drivers are:

1. the 2015 PEEL report from the HMIC into police effectiveness in the area of vulnerability;

2. the National Vulnerability Action Plan in 2020; and

3. the launch of a working definition for all police officers in England and Wales by the College of Policing in 2021.

THE PEEL REPORT 2015: POLICE EFFECTIVENESS – VULNERABILITY

The case studies identified in Table 2.1 between 2000 and 2014, starting from Lord Laming's inquiry report, through to the Jay report in 2014, provide a clear picture of what some may claim to be individual case failings, but which paint a consistent picture of policing in general in connection with vulnerability issues. Policing did not appear to have been prepared for these peripheral issues around vulnerability. The police have proved themselves extremely proficient in '*reacting*' to crime, particularly serious crime, investigating deaths, murders and serious sexual assaults once they have happened, but appeared traditionally stuck within policing models which did not really consider the importance of an individual's personal circumstances in relation to why they were a victim. In some instances, like the Fiona Pilkington case, they failed to piece together the contextual '*pieces of a jigsaw*' when dealing with allegations of crime and anti-social behaviour the family were facing. They also failed to understand the nature of vulnerability in that situation.

The PEEL report in 2015 around police effectiveness in the areas where vulnerability was prevalent was the first real attempt to challenge practices and assess performance in these areas. Previously the HMIC had looked at some '*single issue*' vulnerability matters, for example those related to domestic abuse cases, but the PEEL report of 2015 was the first real scrutiny of dealing with how effective the police were in certain areas as indicated in Table 2.2.

Table 2.2 PEEL inspection framework 2015 (adapted from HMICFRS, 2015)

Inspection title	How effective the police were in protecting vulnerable people from harm and supporting victims
Who was assessed?	• 43 police forces in England and Wales
Areas of focus	• Domestic abuse victims • Missing and absent children • Preparedness to tackle child sexual exploitation
Available gradings	• Outstanding • Good • Requires improvement • Inadequate

The Inspectors undertaking this report used a variety of different methods to examine police effectiveness. These methods included:

- checking data;
- checking force plans and policies;
- examination of case files;
- observation of officers dealing with '*live*' matters;
- interviews with victims;
- interviews with chief officers;
- focus groups with police officers, staff and partners.

Table 2.3 Overview of effectiveness gradings (adapted from HMICFRS, 2015)

Overview of gradings in PEEL report 2015				
Inadequate	**Requires improvement**	**Good**	**Outstanding**	**Total**
4	27	12	0	43

As Table 2.3 illustrates, a simple analysis of the official findings identifies that 31 forces have been found to be ineffective when dealing with matters of vulnerability. While this probably cannot have been a real surprise given the cases from 2000 to 2014 referred to above, it is a pivotal moment in the policing of vulnerability.

The Inspectors did state, however, that:

> *Across the board we found examples of committed and talented officers and staff going above and beyond to meet the needs of vulnerable victims, sometimes in the most difficult of circumstances.*
>
> (HMICFRS, 2015)

Table 2.4 PEEL report 2015: summary of key conclusions

PEEL report 2015: summary of key conclusions		
1	Definition of vulnerability	There was a lack of consistency in how forces defined vulnerability. This led to differences in levels of service and inconsistency around crime recording.
2	Use of risk assessments	Some key differences in completion of risk assessments; some forces preferred to do them by phone rather than in person. Examples of discretion in some forces whether to complete risk assessments or not.
3	Use of THRIVE	Evidence emerged in some forces that it was used to manage demand rather than create a plan suited to the needs of individuals.
4	Investigations	Some evidence of poor staffing in public protection units, and due to this high-risk domestic abuse cases being allocated to non-specialist staff.
5	Compliance with Victims' Code	Considerable evidence of poor updating of victims on the progress of the case. Also, poor consultation with Crown Prosecution Service around the consideration of Special Measures.
6	Partnership working	Some good practices identified around police involvement within MARAC's (multi-agency risk assessment conference) and schools' liaison, but issues with information sharing between partners, and examples of '*silo*' working practices.
7	Domestic abuse	There were noted improvements on the 2014 *Increasingly Everyone's Business* inspection. But inconsistencies remained particularly around the use of the Victims' Code.
8	Missing and absent children	While most forces used the National Police Chiefs' Council definition of absent and missing children, there was evidence of local interpretation. There was also weakness in non-high risk assessment processes and subsequent investigations.
9	Preparedness to tackle CSE	There were examples of good practice, but it was noted to be found where there were skilled and knowledgeable staff provided with clear oversight by supervisors.
10	Final conclusions	The Inspectors recognised that this was a very difficult and problematic area, and that in most cases the police were only one agency and did not have sole responsibility for issues surrounding vulnerability.

Table 2.4 provides a summary of the key conclusions that were reached during the inspection. One of the main observations centres around the diversity of approaches taken by police services around England and Wales. The inspection report recognises some good practice but the police at that point in time did not appear to have the capability to truly share good practice. The College of Policing had been established in 2012, taking over from the National Police Improvement Agency (NPIA), and was slowly working towards establishing a more consistent and professional approach to policing. The next section considers how the College of Policing took responsibility for and drove best practice forward through initiatives such as '*what works*', the use of '*evidence-based policing*' and authorised professional practice as a supportive informative source.

CRITICAL THINKING ACTIVITY 2.2

LEVEL 6

- Take some time to research the PEEL report into police effectiveness in 2015, www.justiceinspectorates.gov.uk/hmicfrs/publications/police-effectiveness-vulnerability-2015/. Find the police service you are a member of, or that are your local force, and click on the link to their specific inspection report in 2015. This will provide you with a benchmark when considering current working practices. It should also allow you to consider where that police service was at the time of the cases between 2000–14.

Sample answers are provided at the end of this book.

THE COLLEGE OF POLICING: INTRODUCTION TO VULNERABILITY-RELATED RISK

This is the second key driver on which this chapter focuses. As discussed earlier, in the past policing has lacked consistency in terms of defining vulnerability and investigating incidents and crimes involving vulnerability, and has struggled with any measure of risk-assessing individuals and their circumstances. In 2021 the College of Policing took responsibility for '*pulling the threads*' together.

As discussed in Chapter 1, a definition of vulnerability was designed based on the THRIVE approach and shared with all police services (THRIVE is a mnemonic which stands for threat, harm, risk, investigation, vulnerability and engagement). This definition had been accepted prior to 2015 but not applied consistently. This was the starting point for the College of Policing when they created their vulnerability-related risk document (College of Policing, 2021a). Their aim was to provide guidelines for police officers, a road map of options based upon best practice and successful outcomes and, more crucially, designed with the thoughts and needs of vulnerable victims in mind.

The College of Policing uses a very simple structure to identify the important elements of approaching vulnerability and risk.

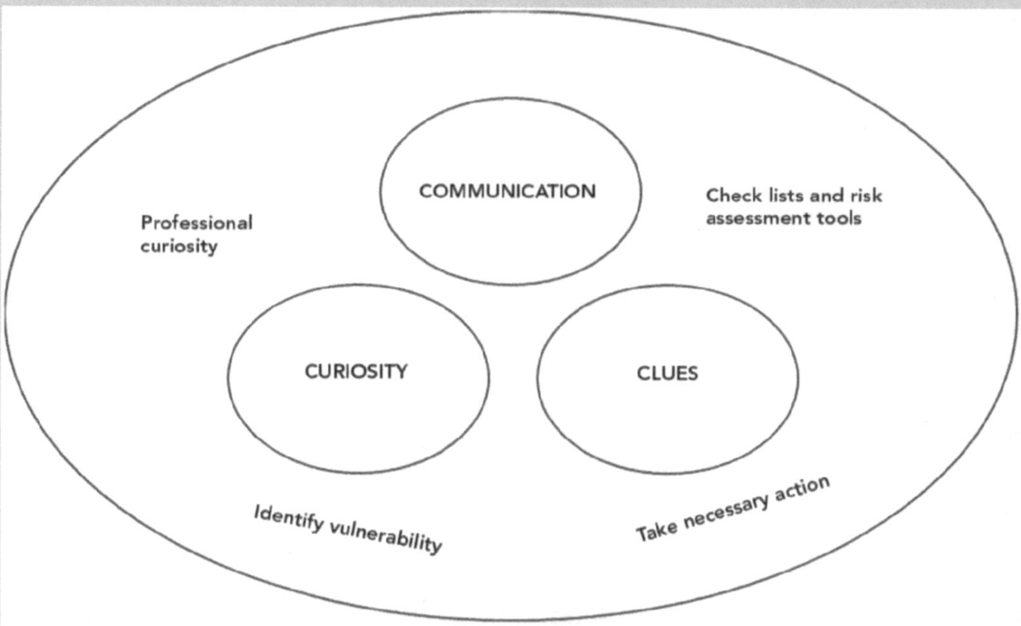

Figure 2.1 College of Policing structure for vulnerability and risk (adapted from College of Policing, 2021a)

The three circles in the centre of Figure 2.1 have no hierarchical structure, but they are each pivotal to investigating an incident where vulnerability exists. To take a simple example from policing, neighbours have contacted the police worried about an elderly lady in the street who gave some money to a '*tradesman*' to fix her roof. The tradesman was knocking door to door, and the neighbours did not believe the roof needed repairing. An allegation of fraud by false representation contrary to section 2 of the Fraud Act 2006 is initially reported as a crime and an officer attends her address.

REFLECTIVE PRACTICE 2.1

LEVEL 4

- You are the attending officer in the example above. Consider the College of Policing structure for vulnerability and risk, and list your thoughts against each of the three headings below.
  - Communication
  - Clues
  - Curiosity
- List five actions that you would take.

Sample answers are provided at the end of this book.

As the attending and investigating officer, it is important that, if you identify vulnerability such as age (an elderly victim), you are professionally curious. Too often police officers can accept this call for service as a '*quick job*', due to the volume of work and unprecedented workloads: one to get the details, do a brief investigation and then file the crimes as '*undetected*' or some similar outcome. What this achieves is a failure to get a '*rich picture*' of crime trends and it potentially isolates a vulnerable victim and places them at risk of becoming a repeat victim and the further harm that may ensue as a result. The concept of repeat victimisation is real and is considered in Chapter 4 in a little more detail.

WHAT DOES PROFESSIONAL CURIOSITY LOOK LIKE?

The College of Policing states that professional curiosity is:

- conducting a proper investigation, asking questions and keeping an open mind;
- not accepting everything at face value – test your understanding, challenge your assumptions;
- being responsible – understanding the need to investigate and take appropriate action.

Why is professional curiosity so important?

> *Professional curiosity means challenging assumptions and exploring and understanding the potentially complex dynamics of a situation, rather than taking things at face value. The literature on coercive control, in particular, shows how perpetrators seek to manipulate situations, and how victims may minimise abuse for a number of reasons, including shame, coercion and threats from the perpetrator.*
>
> (College of Policing, 2021b)

There are several golden threads which weave through this book; professional curiosity is one of the most important ones. It is a mantra for today's police officer to work to, akin to the principles of an investigative mindset which feature prominently in *Criminal Investigation* by Stainton and Ewin (2022). Figure 2.2 below creates a pathway for a new officer to consider the steps which can make up professional curiosity.

STEP 1

- Elicits information from the victim through being professional, diligent and empathetic.

STEP 2

- Encourages disclosure of abuse or harm by the victim.

STEP 3

- Early identification of indicators of vulnerability due to the use of professional curiosity.

STEP 4

- Use of challenge and checking understanding of information.

STEP 5

- Considers circumstances more holistically, considering factors and circumstances which may appear irrelevant such as mental illness or age.

STEP 6

- Thinks outside the box, not beholden to traditional policing solutions which do not always fit every set of circumstances.

STEP 7

- Understands a discrepancy between a risk assessment tool and professional judgement in order to find the best solution for the individual.

STEP 8

- Recognises and uses appropriate steps to gain support from partner agencies for vulnerable individuals.

Figure 2.2 Pathway of professional curiosity (adapted from College of Policing, 2021b)

THE NATIONAL VULNERABILITY ACTION PLAN

The National Vulnerability Action Plan (NVAP) 2020–22 has identified several themes that are present in various strands of vulnerability. The NVAP was devised by the National Police Chiefs' Council (NPCC), which is a body consisting of all Chief Constables in England and Wales.

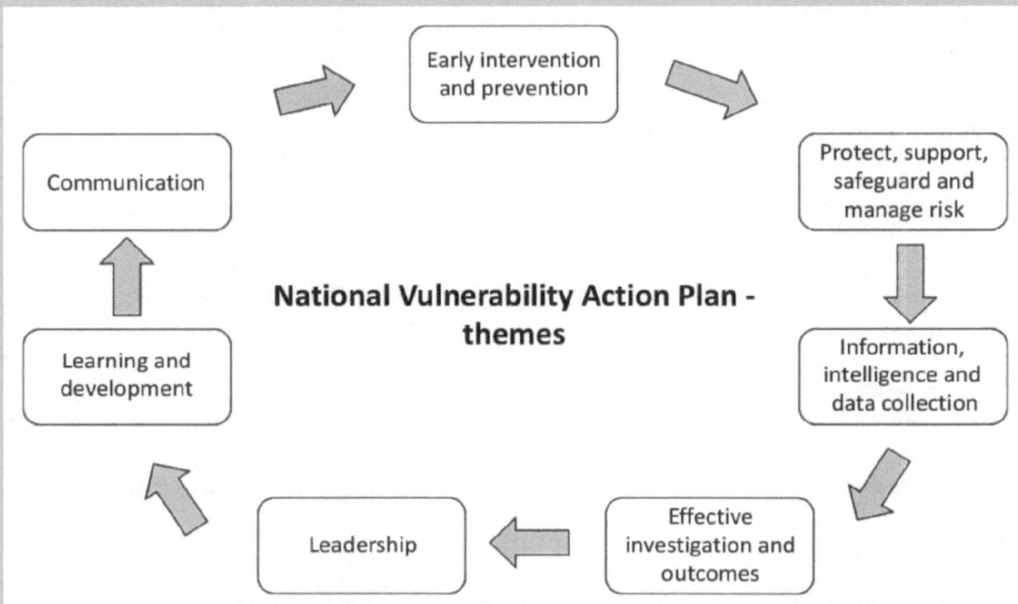

Figure 2.3 NVAP themes (adapted from VKPP, 2023)

The alignment between the vulnerability and risk work of the College of Policing and the NPCC is clearly not accidental and marks a clear intent to deal with the historical shortcomings in relation to individuals who display vulnerability traits. The seven NVAP themes illustrated in Figure 2.3 provide a complete and purposeful approach to dealing with an individual who has a vulnerability and is victim of a crime. The links between the NVAP themes and the pathway steps of professional curiosity are clearly linked. Table 2.5 highlights the comparable points between the two areas.

Table 2.5 Comparison of links between the NVAP themes and the steps of professional curiosity

NVAP theme	Professional curiosity step	Comment
Learning and development	Step 5	Police officers should be fully trained in dealing with vulnerability and risk as an addition to their knowledge of their powers and criminal offences.
Communication	Steps 1, 2, 3 and 7	Officers should communicate appropriately with victims, building a rapport that will allow the earliest possible intervention and, if possible, prevention of becoming a victim in the first place.
Safeguarding	Step 8	This will allow the officer and appropriate agencies to safeguard the individual, through partnership approaches to safeguarding.
Intelligence	Step 1	The submission of intelligence and information gathered during the investigation will create a rich picture against the perpetrators.
Investigation	Steps 4 and 5	A full and encompassing investigation can achieve a positive outcome such as a charge to court.

The final theme is leadership. The importance of supervision and leadership within policing cannot be overemphasised. There was no leadership step in the professional curiosity pathway, but it is vital that supervisors and leaders accept responsibility for ensuring these areas receive best practice and a highly professional approach. Part of this supervision is recognising and trusting officers to make the right calls around vulnerable individuals pertinent to the risk assessment and finding a specific solution to that individual case.

POLICING SPOTLIGHT

The NVAP considers a plethora of policing areas where improvements are necessary. One of them relates to mental health. Action 2.1.2 of the action plan recognises the impact of mental health issues across the whole range of vulnerabilities and recommends that as part of any assessment, mental health needs should be considered. The action plan clearly stipulates that appropriate signposting and guidance be made available by the police officer to the vulnerable person.

The action plan (2.1.2) highlights three objectives:

→

1. that appropriate and consistent use be made of the NPCC definition of a mental health-related incident (MHRI);
2. the need to understand the cause of each incident in order to be able to identify specific mental health issues and to determine links to other vulnerabilities within the THRIVE approach;
3. the need to evaluate any mental health indicators when dealing with victims, offenders or members of the public and signpost to the appropriate organisation or agency for support.

The NVAP incorporates the research of the mental health charity MIND where it has been identified that individuals with mental health issues are three times more likely to be victims of crime (MIND, 2018). The NVAP also considers the impact of multiple adversaries on individuals, including issues such as:

- disability;
- social exclusion;
- discrimination;
- poverty;
- unemployment;
- homelessness;
- self-neglect;
- substance misuse.

This theme of adversaries is considered in more detail in Chapter 4. It is sufficient to state here that becoming a victim of crime can be both predictable and complex, but research has revealed individuals who experience multiple adversaries and consequently mental health issues are far more likely to become victims of crime.

POLICING VULNERABILITY: KEY LEGISLATIVE DRIVERS FOR CHANGE

In the last 25 years, further key drivers for change in how police can deal with issues of vulnerability can be found in a series of legislative changes. Lessons from various serious case reviews, inquiries and other forms of scrutiny have led to the legislators devising new acts of Parliament and other guidance to support the police and its partner agencies in improving approaches for identifying and dealing with vulnerability.

CRITICAL THINKING ACTIVITY 2.3

LEVEL 5

As a result of perceived and actual failings, the police and partner agencies have been evolving in terms of how they respond and deal with often complex situations involving vulnerable victims.

- Identify three pieces of legislation in England and Wales which have been enacted in the last 25 years that have assisted the police and partners to improve the service of safeguarding vulnerable victims.

Sample answers are provided at the end of this book.

Table 2.6 below highlights several pieces of legislation and guidance documents all from the last 25 years. Hopefully you will have identified three of them in the above activity.

Table 2.6 Key drivers for change: legislation to assist the policing of vulnerability

Year	Legislation (post 1999)	Relevance
1999	Youth Justice and Criminal Evidence Act	Introduction of special measures to support vulnerable and intimidated witnesses.
2003	Sexual Offences Act	Sarah's Law – Child Sex Offender Disclosure Scheme.
2004	Children Act	Based around themes of safety and security for children.
2005	Mental Capacity Act	Legislation to support an individual making their own decisions unless they are unable to, and safeguards being put in place.
2006	Safeguarding Vulnerable Groups Act	New legislation around barred lists and vetting requirements in relation to working with vulnerable individuals.
2010	Equality Act	Creation of protected characteristics.
2014	Care Act	National care and support for adults and children.
2015	Serious Crime Act	Specific legislation for protection from female genital mutilation, sexual exploitation, sexual communication and cruelty.
2015	Mental Health Act (Code of Practice)	A code of practice to support mental health legislation.

Table 2.6 *(continued)*

Year	Legislation (post 1999)	Relevance
2015	Modern Slavery Act	To combat offences of modern slavery, incorporating previous offences relating to trafficking and slavery.
2018	Working together to safeguard children	Provides statutory guidance on partnership working to safeguard children.
2021	Domestic Abuse Act	Clare's Law – Domestic Violence Disclosure Scheme.

Chapter 1 looked at the Care Act 2014 and the Mental Capacity Act 2005. This chapter looks in more detail at:

- Safeguarding Vulnerable Groups Act 2006;
- Sexual Offences Act 2003, aka Sarah's Law;
- Domestic Abuse Act 2021, aka Clare's Law.

It illustrates how these pieces of legislation assist the police and its partners when working with vulnerable individuals. The forthcoming chapters explore and examine other pieces of legislation such as the Modern Slavery Act 2015.

HOW DOES THE SAFEGUARDING VULNERABLE GROUPS ACT 2006 IMPACT ON POLICING VULNERABILITY?

The Safeguarding Vulnerable Groups Act 2006 was borne out of recommendation 19 of the Bichard inquiry into the Soham murders. It resulted in the creation of a registration scheme for anyone wishing to work with children or vulnerable adults. The police are required and will be requested to consider each applicant against intelligence it holds in its systems. A decision will be made by the regulatory body, the Disclosure and Barring Service (DBS), as to whether the police intelligence is sufficient to refuse to issue a registration certificate to work with either children or vulnerable adults. The implication for vulnerable individuals is that the police and partner agencies conduct a closer examination of those applying to and working with vulnerable groups, and as a result it is unlikely that individuals like Ian Huntley will ever again be employed in positions of trust.

HOW DOES SARAH'S LAW IMPACT ON POLICING VULNERABILITY?

The Sexual Offences Act 2003 created the Child Sex Offender Disclosure Scheme or what has become known as Sarah's Law. Sarah's Law followed the kidnap and murder of Sarah Payne in 2000 by a convicted sex offender, Roy Whiting, who lived close to Sarah. First trialled in 2008, it was fully integrated into policing in England and Wales by 2010. It allows parents, grandparents or family friends to ask the police whether a person who has contact with a child has a record for child sexual offences or poses a risk to the child. If the police determine that such a risk exists, they must consider informing the parents or guardians. It is a proactive process which allows concerned parents to seek information about individuals who are close by, if they have child sex convictions and are considered a risk.

HOW DOES CLARE'S LAW IMPACT ON POLICING VULNERABILITY?

Clare's Law was derived from the Domestic Violence Disclosure Scheme, which gives anyone a right to ask the police if they believe that they or someone they know is in a relationship with an individual who could be abusive towards them. The scheme is named after Clare Wood, who was murdered by an abusive former partner in 2009. This is another vital piece of legislation which aims to protect victims of domestic abuse and affords proactive means for vulnerable partners to find out if a new or prospective partner has a history of intimate partner violence.

The three pieces of legislation discussed above are important in that they demonstrate a desire not only to learn from past mistakes, but also attempt to avoid other vulnerable victims from becoming targeted. Victim precipitation and lifestyle theories of victimology will be examined in more detail in Chapter 4, but they are both challenged to a strong degree by these pieces of legislation.

THE CONCEPT OF RISK IN RELATION TO POLICING VULNERABLE INDIVIDUALS

Chapter 1 introduced the concept of risk in the context of the definition of harm, and the risk of harm, and then again as part of the THRIVE model. Being able to assess risk is a major part of modern policing, and particularly so within the area of policing vulnerable individuals. The College of Policing has created guidelines to assist officers in spotting signs associated with vulnerability. The attending or investigating officer can be in contact with an individual who is at risk of harm or has suffered harm, and as such the officer needs to conduct a risk assessment to determine the level and likelihood of risk. The College of Policing produced ten risk principles for officers to consider. These risk principles, which feature in Table 2.7 below, should be considered as part of the decision-making process through the national decision model (NDM) (College of Policing, 2013a). The NDM has distinct stages an officer will rotate through while assessing a situation. The stages are as follows:

- gathering information and intelligence;
- assessing the risk and developing a working strategy;
- considering powers, policies and procedures;
- identifying options and contingencies;
- taking action and reviewing what has happened.

The NDM is cyclical and the rotation around the stages can continue for some time.

POLICING SPOTLIGHT

In the area of mental health issues, a structured assessment framework was devised to assist officers to identify vulnerability. Dr Karen Wright and Ivan McGlen at the University of Central Lancashire created the Vulnerability Assessment Framework (VAF) which they stated could be incorporated into the gathering information and intelligence stage of the NDM (Wright and McGlen, 2012).

Officers can build a more precise and detailed record of the circumstances that led them to identify someone as vulnerable and in need of either assistance, arrest or referral. Officers follow a simple ABCDE system of recording information, which is then easily transferable to other agencies.

The ABCDE system is as follows.

- *Appearance and atmosphere – what you see first, including physical problems such as injuries.*
- *Behaviour – what individuals are doing, and if this is appropriate behaviour given the situation.*
- *Communication – what individuals say and how they say it.*
- *Danger – whether individuals are in danger and whether their actions put other people in danger.*
- *Environment – where they are situated, whether anyone else is there and what impact the wider circumstances may have on the individual's health and safety.*

(College of Policing, 2021c)

The VAF is a very useful tool of assessment for police officers; while it has clearly been adapted from its original purpose within medical circumstances, it provides officers with an astute and easy to remember assessment tool.

HOW ARE THE RISK PRINCIPLES RELEVANT TO VULNERABILITY?

To the new police officer, assessing risk will probably be a daunting process to follow. Traditionally, like many of its partner agencies, policing can tend to be risk averse. Through their ten risk principles (see Table 2.7) the College of Policing encourages police to have:

> *a more positive approach to risk by openly supporting decision makers and building their confidence in taking risks.*

(College of Policing, 2013b)

Police officers are encouraged to use the risk principles in conjunction with the NDM.

Table 2.7 The risk principles (adapted from the College of Policing, 2013b)

	Principle	Observation
1	The willingness to make decisions in conditions of uncertainty.	One of the core requirements of policing. The need to take risks rather than avoid them.
2	Assessing the risk to maintaining or achieving the safety, security and well-being of individuals.	The risk to police reputation is secondary to the primary responsibility to protect life.
3	A good risk decision involves judgement and balance.	The balance is between the benefits of the decision and the likelihood of harm and its seriousness.
4	Understanding that harm can never be totally prevented.	As a result, decisions regarding risk should be judged by the quality of the decision, not the outcome.
5	Difficult to make risk decisions, can be affected by numerous factors and influences.	These factors and influences can be both formal and informal.
6	There is a standard expected when making a risk decision.	The same decision should have been made by an officer of the same length of service or experience.
7	Recording decisions regarding risk is a matter of judgement.	Not all decisions need to be recorded, considering the likelihood and seriousness of harm being caused.
8	Avoiding becoming risk averse.	Policing needs to develop a culture of learning from both successes and failures. Good risk taking should be recognised and shared.
9	Good risk decisions depend upon having good quality information.	It is vital that the police and partners share relevant information about risk and those at risk.
10	Risk decisions should be consistently made in line with the principles.	An officer who makes decisions in line with the principles should be encouraged and supported by the organisation.

EVIDENCE-BASED POLICING

All police officers undertake a one-day vulnerability and risk programme as part of their wider training requirements. This programme has been designed as a result of an aspiration to learn lessons from the failures and errors of the past when dealing with individuals with vulnerabilities. The

Independent Office for Police Conduct (IOPC) reported the development of this training in its magazine *Learning the Lessons* in 2018.

> *The training package supports a culture change in forces, encouraging frontline officers and staff to look beyond the obvious and feel empowered to use their professional curiosity when dealing with those who are vulnerable.*
>
> (IOPC, 2018)

The training programme is extremely pertinent when considered in the context of drivers for change. It seeks to endorse a '*universal definition*' of vulnerability within policing using the THRIVE approach. Officers are encouraged to use their '*professional curiosity*' and identify signs of vulnerability early. It also emphasises the importance of safeguarding and recognises that the police are only one part of the vulnerability jigsaw.

REASONS FOR AN INCREASED DEMAND FOR POLICE SERVICES ARISING FROM THE REPORTING OF CHILD SEX ABUSE

The children's charity the NSPCC recorded a 57 per cent increase in recorded offences against children between 2014–15 and 2019–20 (NSPCC, 2020). In the period 2019–20, it identified 73,518 recorded offences which included offences of online grooming and sexual assaults against children. In addition, the NSPCC report in 2020 detailed that:

- girls were four times more likely to be victims than boys;
- the most common age for children to report crimes was 14 years old;
- there were 12,374 sex crimes recorded as being committed against children under 10 years old.

There are several reasons why this increase in reporting of child sex abuse occurred. One of the main factors is believed to be '*the Savile effect*'. This relates to the reports of historic sexual abuse perpetrated by Jimmy Savile. Savile was well known as a children's television star and charity fundraiser. Following his death in 2011, hundreds of allegations of sex abuse by Savile were made. Such a multitude of allegations led the police to consider Savile to be an extreme sexual predator.

POLICING SPOTLIGHT

In October 2012 Operation Yewtree was launched. It followed a television documentary which made allegations against Jimmy Savile. The ITV documentary *Exposure: The Other Side of Jimmy Savile* focused on claims of sexual abuse perpetrated on children by Jimmy Savile. Operation Yewtree was headed by the Metropolitan Police and initially focused on the allegations against Jimmy Savile. The operation gradually expanded two further strands of investigation, into the historic sexual abuse allegations against Savile and his associates, and into similar historic allegations against others. The Savile effect was clearly a pivotal moment for many '*silenced*' victims of sexual abuse.

The Yewtree investigation attracted considerable media attention and coverage. Once the magnitude of victim numbers became known, there followed a backlash against numerous public bodies for allegedly '*covering up*' the crimes of Savile. Bodies such as the police, National Health Service (NHS), the Department of Health, the British Broadcasting Company (BBC) and the Crown Prosecution Service (CPS) were all heavily criticised and tarnished with the '*must have known*' or the failure to take allegations seriously brushes; after all, Savile was a national celebrity and charity fundraiser extraordinaire, fêted by most of those organisations.

Operation Yewtree determined that allegations against Savile spanned six decades and involved victims between the ages of 5 and 75. Specifically, many allegations centred around 28 NHS hospitals which were identified as locations for sexual abuse, and the facility at Broadmoor psychiatric hospital was also found to be included in Savile's area of influence.

Operation Yewtree determined that Savile had been under investigation by three forces while he was alive, and that he should have been charged with several offences. While perhaps Operation Yewtree did not bring Savile to justice for his crimes, it did result in convictions for many other individuals such as Paul Gadd (Gary Glitter), Max Clifford and Rolf Harris, to name but three (Operation Yewtree, 2011).

Following the success of Operation Yewtree, other police investigations originated. In the summer of 2014, Operation Hydrant examined historic allegations of child sex abuse. It had approximately 1400 suspects under investigation, over 250 of which were in the '*public eye*', including other television celebrities, members of religious institutions and children's home staff. In November 2014 Operation Midland, a specific investigation, started that focused on allegations against high-profile British citizens including former Members of Parliament, Harvey Proctor and Leon Brittan.

While police investigations against Savile were the catalyst which generated both the confidence and enthusiasm of victims of sexual abuse to make their allegations and have their '*story told*', Operation Midland was a specular failure. The outcome was potentially to hinder victims coming forward. Confidence in the police to investigate fairly was seriously hampered when they used a '*victim*' called Carl Beech, who it was subsequently proved lied comprehensively. However, there were serious failings in the investigation, where the investigating officer had not utilised the principles of professional curiosity by:

- not conducting a proper investigation, asking questions and keeping an open mind;
- accepting everything at face value;
- failing to be responsible.

In 2016, Beech was imprisoned for a total of 18 years for perverting the course of justice and other paedophile offences (Henriques 2016).

The confidence in the police to investigate historic sex abuse allegations following the death of Savile also coincided with improved police recording and investigation of such crimes. The scandals of and subsequent investigations into child sexual abuse in Rochdale and Rotherham (1997–2013) were also another '*encouraging*' reason for other victims to report crimes against themselves by predators and grooming perpetrators. Following the abhorrence of Rochdale and Rotherham, the government made child sex abuse a '*priority*' and as big a national threat as serious and organised crime.

In 2017 the CPS claimed that they were prosecuting more offenders for sex crimes than ever before. They claimed that 13,700 convictions were obtained for all sexual offences, including rape. They were also able to determine that the ages of rape victims were as follows:

- 52 per cent of victims were under the age of 24;
- 18 per cent of victims were aged between 14–17 years old;
- 9 per cent of victims were aged under 13.

While it is a complex question to answer in relation to the reasons for the increase in recording of historic child sexual abuse offences, it is clear from the '*Jimmy Savile effect*' that the demands on the police and some of its partner agencies became incredibly onerous. It is also clear that in the past, the police were not in a position to always deal professionally with vulnerable individuals.

SUMMARY OF KEY CONCEPTS

Having read this chapter you should now be aware that policing individuals with vulnerability factors as victims of crime has been far from successful historically, but that lessons have been learnt and improvements made. The key concepts covered included the following:

- how lessons learnt have informed the current policing position in relation to policing vulnerability and risk;
- how new legislative changes have supported the police and other agencies to support those with vulnerabilities;
- the importance of the PEEL report of 2015 which has improved police responses;
- the importance of the principle of professional curiosity;
- the concept of understanding risk in relation to policing vulnerable individuals;
- the reasons for an increased demand for police services arising from the reporting of child sex abuse.

CHECK YOUR KNOWLEDGE

1. What was the relevance of the Mental Capacity Act 2005?
2. What is professional curiosity?
3. Name five key conclusions of the 2015 PEEL report on the effectiveness of the police response to vulnerability.
4. What are the three objectives in relation to mental health in the National Vulnerability Action Plan of 2020?
5. How do either Sarah's Law or Clare's Law impact on policing vulnerability?

Sample answers are provided at the end of this book.

FURTHER READING

Introduction to vulnerability-related risk. Available at: www.college.police.uk/guidance/vulnerability-related-risks/introduction-vulnerability-related-risk. The College of Policing guidance provided in relation to dealing with vulnerability is a valuable resource for all officers.

CHAPTER 3

INCREASED VULNERABILITY: INTRINSIC AND EXTRINSIC FACTORS

LEARNING OBJECTIVES

AFTER READING THIS CHAPTER YOU WILL BE ABLE TO:

- **explain the impact of intrinsic factors on vulnerability;**
- **explain the impact of extrinsic factors on vulnerability;**
- **discuss how intrinsic and extrinsic factors combine to increase the risk of harm;**
- **examine the outcomes where intrinsic and extrinsic factors are not identified by professional curiosity during an investigation.**

INTRODUCTION

The establishment of a definition of vulnerability for policing, albeit after a problematic history of dealing with vulnerable individuals, and the understanding of the key national drivers, both in terms of lessons learnt and legislative and policy developments made, may suggest that it will be a simple matter now to label the factors and reasons why an individual may be vulnerable. The cases highlighted in Chapter 2 can mostly be attributed to one vulnerability factor. The case of Daniel Pelka, for example, was related to his status as a young child, while Fiona Pilkington's daughter Francesca was due to her special educational needs. It would be easy to accept this simple formula to understand the issue of individuals with vulnerabilities being identified and targeted due to a single factor, but this chapter considers the complexity of vulnerability.

Another consideration which needs to be discussed is the manner in which vulnerability was viewed by the police and others before the College of Policing's definition of vulnerability in 2021. Is it possible to look through these previous lenses to determine actual vulnerability? This could allow for an analysis as to why the police in particular, but also their partner agencies, were guilty of so many failures when it came to their duties of care.

INTERPRETATIONS OF VULNERABILITY PRIOR TO 2021

It is important to consider the College of Policing THRIVE definition of vulnerability again before we consider the journey that policing has taken.

> *[A] person is vulnerable if, as a result of their situation or circumstances, they are unable to take care of or protect themselves from harm or exploitation.*
>
> (College of Policing, 2021a)

Researchers and criminologists reveal that policing previously did consider the issue of vulnerability. The police had a very one-dimensional interpretation of vulnerability which was not borne out of a wide consideration of factors but limited due to certain criteria. Killias and Clerici (2000, p 437) stated:

> *Physical vulnerability seems to play an important and consistent role in the genesis of the fear of crime.*

This is an interesting viewpoint as vulnerability was considered a result of certain physical characteristics rather than a wider sense of personal vulnerable factors, or even as a result of environmental or situational factors. Jackson (2009) agreed with this synopsis that the focus on vulnerability related to age and gender. In their research, Killias and Clerici (2000) identify a key link between the fear of crime and subsequent identification of a vulnerability factor. One of their research areas examined walking at night. Their results appeared to suggest that everyone would conduct a personal risk assessment before walking at night. The results generally identified age and gender as being the two main factors of vulnerability. Therefore, a female would be more likely to fear crime when walking at night than a male.

Another study by Bartkowiak-Théron and Asquith (2012) in the context of Australian policing also recognised that policing was only just slowly moving from a traditional standpoint where age and gender were the two readily recognisable vulnerability factors. Does this traditional and restrictive interpretation of what constituted vulnerability explain the failings of the police as outlined in the incidents in Table 2.1? Policing is traditional and slow to change, often reacting to situations as opposed to proactively anticipating them. This is further exacerbated by the role of intersectionality within vulnerability which adds a further level to the complexity. Intersectionality in this context can be seen as the vulnerable person or persons being affected by discrimination and disadvantaged as a result of their vulnerability in the particular context of the criminal activity they are facing.

CRITICAL THINKING ACTIVITY 3.1

LEVEL 4

- Reflecting on the first two chapters, consider how a person could be vulnerable to being a victim of crime. List five personal factors (other than age or gender) that could make an individual vulnerable to becoming a victim of crime and explain briefly why.

Sample answers are provided at the end of this book.

You should have produced five personal factors which could make an individual vulnerable to becoming a victim of crime. Figure 3.1 provides a quick overview of some personal factors which could, in certain circumstances, lead to or make an individual vulnerable to harm or the risk of harm.

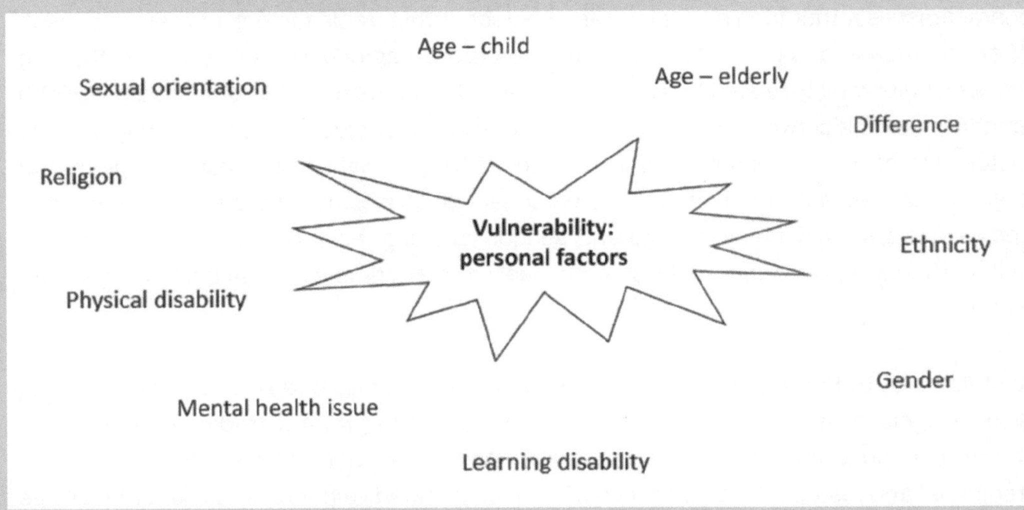

Figure 3.1 Vulnerability: personal factors

As discussed earlier, it is important to note that a person's vulnerability does not need to be permanent but could be temporary. It is also possible that an individual with one or more of these personal factors may not be vulnerable at all. This point will be discussed later.

INTRINSIC FACTORS OF VULNERABILITY

Table 3.1 below considers each of the personal factors which could make someone vulnerable and links them to case studies or considerations in terms of reasoning. Consider the list you created in Critical thinking activity 3.1 and read Table 3.1.

Table 3.1 An examination of personal factors

Personal factor	Description	Case studies
Age – child	An individual is vulnerable due to their young years.	Victoria Climbié Peter Connelly (Baby P) Daniel Pelka Rochdale child sex gangs Rotherham child sex gangs

Table 3.1 (*continued*)

Personal factor	Description	Case studies
Age – elderly	An individual is vulnerable due to their senior years.	Often socially isolated, living in urban areas, with reliance on public transport and with consistent behaviour patterns. Elderly victims of the Tunbridge Wells burglar David Wells.
Difference	An individual is vulnerable due to being different in their lifestyle choices.	Sophie Lancaster made a lifestyle choice which was different to others. This difference in appearance attracted hateful comments and tragically a violent assault which led to her death.
Ethnicity	An individual is vulnerable due to their ethnicity.	Men from mixed ethnic backgrounds (21 per cent) were more likely to be victims of crime than men from any other ethnic group for the three years from April 2017 to March 2020. Bijan Ebrahimi
Gender	An individual is vulnerable due to their gender.	Women are considerably more likely to experience repeated and severe forms of abuse, including sexual violence. They are also more likely to have experienced sustained physical, psychological or emotional abuse, or violence which results in injury or death. A recent example was Sarah Everard.
Learning disability	An individual is vulnerable due to a learning disability.	Francesca Hardwick Fiona Pilkington
Mental health issue	An individual is vulnerable due to a mental health issue.	IOPC *Learning the Lessons*, number 34 (2019). Case study where police misinterpreted and mishandled a call for assistance, leading to the death of a vulnerable male. Vulnerable victim of rapist Robert Hassell.
Physical disability	An individual is vulnerable due to physical disability.	There is no offence of disability hate crime per se, but section 66 Sentencing Act 2020 states at the time of committing the offence, or immediately before or after doing so, the offender demonstrated towards the victim of the offence hostility based on a disability (or presumed disability) of the victim; or the offence was motivated (wholly or partly) by hostility towards persons who have a disability or a particular disability. Bijan Ebrahimi.

→

Table 3.1 *(continued)*

Personal factor	Description	Case studies
Religion	An individual is vulnerable due to their religious beliefs.	From UK government data between 2018 to 2019, the police recorded 8566 hate crime offences related to religion; these offences accounted for 8 per cent of all hate crimes recorded by the police. Bijan Ebrahimi
Sexual orientation	An individual is vulnerable due to their sexual orientation.	Stop Hate UK recorded that in 2020/21 sexual orientation hate crimes increased from 15,972 to 17,135. Morgan Fevre

Each of the personal factors listed above can be considered as factors which could cause an individual to be vulnerable. If you consider age in relation to a child, for example, you can see a whole range of case studies where the age of the individual was clearly the main factor in their vulnerability. The tragic cases of Victoria Climbié, Baby P and Daniel Pelka are clear examples. The incidences of child sexual abuse in Rochdale and Rotherham are also examples of how children are vulnerable during their early years.

INTRINSIC FACTORS: CASE STUDY 1

An independent report by Professor Alexis Jay, released in 2014, examined the circumstances which surrounded the estimated 1400 cases of children being sexually exploited between 1997 and 2013. The inquiry investigated the roles of South Yorkshire Police and the social services. The findings reported are horrific, describing among many things the appalling abuse including rape of girls as young as 11 by large numbers of male perpetrators. It also describes how young girls were trafficked to other northern English towns for purposes of sexual abuse and it highlights how they were abducted, beaten, threatened, intimidated and sexually abused.

The report found a collective failure of leadership in the first 12 years of the offences taking place in both the police and the social services. While social care leaders downplayed the scale and seriousness of the allegations, the police did not prioritise child sexual exploitation (CSE) and treated many victims with contempt, frequently failing to act on allegations of abuse. There was an extremely damaging factor which hindered the initial investigations into the claims: the police and social services feared being labelled racist. While most of the victims were young white females, the perpetrators were mainly Asian adult males. An apparent '*genuine*' concern over causing issues for community cohesion in and around Rotherham was cited to explain the poor responses of the police and social services.

An interesting interpretation into police failings was made by the new Police and Crime Commissioner (PCC) Alan Billings, who told the BBC:

> *It is not about girls who are out of control, who are disrespectful of authority, who are incorrigible in their behaviour ... it is about young people who are victims.*
>
> (BBC, 2015)

Billings accepted that the police had not recognised '*grooming*' as taking place. In terms of the context of how the police were failing vulnerable victims, the Jay report and the comments of the PCC point to failures of training and a lack of recognition of the seriousness of the offences under the banner of CSE.

POLICING SPOTLIGHT

Following the inquiry into allegations of child sexual abuse in Rotherham, one of the consequences of the Jay report (2014) was the instigation of Operation Stovewood by the National Crime Agency (NCA). The investigation was requested by the Chief Constable of South Yorkshire Police. The NCA stated that their priorities were as follows:

> *Operation Stovewood is a unique and unprecedented investigation with hundreds of potential victims.*
>
> *It is those* ***victims who are the focus*** *of the investigation, and our first priority is to provide them with the best possible support and advice, often through working with our partners.*
>
> *Our second priority is seek to* ***identify and bring offenders to justice****, prioritising those who may still be active in Rotherham or elsewhere today and those who have caused most harm in the past.*
>
> *Our third priority is to work with local partners and communities to* ***rebuild public confidence*** *in agencies. We know many victims feel let down by their experiences previously. We aim to do the best we can to rectify that.*
>
> (NCA, 2022)

In terms of regaining public trust and confidence and addressing the historic failings, the involvement of the NCA was a shrewd approach to investigating the allegations of mass historic child sexual abuse. The NCA was an independent agency untainted by the failures of early investigations into complaints. The impact of Operation Stovewood is still being felt by perpetrators in 2022, as the NCA stated there were 40 '*separate*' investigations ongoing in June 2022 when a press release announced that a 57-year-old man was charged with a series of sexual offences against four females aged from 15–19 between 1996 and 1999 (NCA, 2022).

INTRINSIC FACTORS: CASE STUDY 2

A second case study involving the murder of Bijan Ebrahimi in Bristol in 2013 is now considered. In terms of individual vulnerability factors, this case study is interesting. Bijan was an Iranian refugee living in the Brislington area of Bristol. In terms of his vulnerability factors there were three possible issues which made him vulnerable. Bijan was:

1. an Iranian – nationality and an immigrant;
2. physically disabled;
3. a non-Christian religious believer.

These three factors were all considered by the Independent Office for Police Conduct (IOPC) who investigated the failings of Avon and Somerset Police into the murder of Bijan on 16 July 2013.

A brief overview of the case of Bijan was that, over a period of seven years, he was persecuted by neighbours as being a suspected paedophile. During that time Bijan made 73 calls to the police. These calls included allegations of racial abuse, criminal damage and threats to kill. Bijan became considered to be a nuisance to the police, and to some officers a liar, tainting their views on his allegations. The police appeared to accept the viewpoints of neighbours completely, and largely dismissed Bijan's allegations. Among the evidence from the calls made by Bijan was an arson attack on his property which resulted in him having to be relocated, and the word '*paedo*' being scrawled on his door. Three days before his death Bijan was arrested by police following an allegation that he had been taking photographs of children. Following a short investigation, the allegation was found to be without foundation, and Bijan was released.

Bijan was beaten to death by a neighbour called Lee James on 16 July and subsequently his body was set on fire. Following Bijan's death, a referral was made to the IOPC. Their investigation produced some troubling conclusions for the way Bijan's allegations had been handled by the police.

The case of Bijan Ebrahimi has troubling echoes of the case of Fiona Pilkington which was discussed in Chapter 1. There is a pattern of allegations which do not always appear to be linked together, and the consequence of the police's failure to deal with matters professionally and appropriately led to tragic deaths in both cases.

Table 3.2 IOPC findings Bijan Ebrahimi

	IOPC finding	Comments
1	Systematic failure to apply national and local legislation, policies and procedures.	The main overwhelming conclusion was that Avon and Somerset Police had systematically failed Bijan over the course of the seven years leading up to his death.
2	Inconsistency around reporting crimes alleged by Bijan.	Bijan had made 73 calls alleging crimes against himself. There were 40 failures to record a crime.
3	Failure to identify hate crimes being perpetrated against Bijan.	Bijan appeared never to have been recognised as a victim of hate crime. The IOPC asserted that 31 crimes should have been reported as hate crimes.
4	Failure to identify Bijan as a repeat victim.	There was no apparent recognition that Bijan was a repeat victim.
5	Failure to identify Bijan as a vulnerable person.	Since there was a failure to identify many of the offences as being hate crimes and being perpetrated against the same victim, there was no consideration that Bijan may be vulnerable. The IOPC found evidence that officers saw Bijan's victimisation negatively and considered him to be a nuisance, liar or attention seeker.

The IOPC findings summarised in Table 3.2 identify clear threads where failures have occurred.

- The difficulty of identifying an individual's vulnerability is a golden thread from the historic review of cases where lessons need to be learnt.
- The inability to identify repeat victimisation emerges again. Chapter 4 considers repeat victimisation in more detail.
- What the IOPC describes as '*systematic failures*' in police systems and approaches is another golden thread when looking at how police had handled these types of matter in the past.
- Another conclusion which needs identifying and is so pertinent to so many of the case studies where failures occurred is the importance of supervision.

The IOPC report into the death of Bijan ended:

> *The failure to do so cannot be laid at the door of one officer, or even the Neighbourhood Policing Team. The extent of the failures and the degree to which they were apparent to others, including supervisors, are such that it might reasonably be said that the Avon and Somerset Constabulary, as an institution, must at least share the responsibility.*
>
> (IPCC, 2014)

The IOPC investigation led to the CPS prosecuting four officers and the following outcomes resulted. One officer, PC Duffy, and a Police Community Support Officer (PCSO), PCSO Passmore, were jailed for their failures in handling Bijan's complaints, both for Misconduct in a Public Office. Two further officers, PCs Harris and Winter, were found not guilty at the trial, but were subsequently dismissed by Avon and Somerset Police for their failings. These findings illustrate the vital importance of police officers using professional curiosity and making professional judgements based upon recent training which ensure their knowledge and understanding of vulnerability issues is current.

EXTRINSIC FACTORS OF VULNERABILITY

Extrinsic factors include two main subcategories:

1. situational factors;
2. incidental factors.

CRITICAL THINKING ACTIVITY 3.2

LEVEL 5

Previously in Chapter 1 you were tasked to identify situations and circumstances in Critical thinking activity 1.2 which may render someone vulnerable and at risk of harm. What other situations and what other types of incidents could be factors which could make an individual vulnerable to becoming a victim of crime?

- List three new situations and three new incidents which you believe could be a factor and briefly explain why.

Sample answers are provided at the end of this book.

Table 3.3 identifies a series of factors which could be situational or incidental to an individual becoming a victim. Situational vulnerability factors could include where the impact of crime is increased because of where it happens, such as areas which are socially or economically deprived neighbourhoods or already have high crime rates. Incidental vulnerability factors include where an incident of crime is likely to induce negative effects for victims, such as the experience of repeated occurrences or where victims may believe they are being targeted personally.

Table 3.3 Extrinsic factors

Extrinsic factor	Description	Comments
Adverse childhood experiences (ACEs)	Adverse Childhood Experiences (ACEs) are '*highly stressful, and potentially traumatic, events or situations that occur during childhood and/or adolescence.* *They can be a single event, or prolonged threats to, and breaches of, the young person's safety, security, trust or bodily integrity*' (Young Minds, 2018).	ACEs can include: • physical abuse; • sexual abuse; • emotional abuse; • living with someone who abused drugs; • living with someone who abused alcohol; • exposure to domestic violence; • living with someone who has gone to prison; • living with someone with serious mental illness; • losing a parent through divorce, death or abandonment.
Adverse community environments	Often linked to ACEs, there can be factors which will hinder an individual's development or possibly highlight a pathway to negative outcomes.	They can include: • poverty; • discrimination; • community disruption; • lack of opportunity, work, financial remuneration etc; • poor housing; • use of or victim of violence.
Adverse cultural influences	Despite the existence of a multicultural society, there are still examples of negative interpretations of different cultures.	One recognisable example is the labelling of certain cultural and often religious groups in negative ways.

→

Table 3.3 (*continued*)

Extrinsic factor	Description	Comments
Coercive control	Coercive control as a phrase is largely connected to domestic abuse law. It is an act or a pattern of acts of assault, threats, humiliation and intimidation or other abuse that is used to harm, punish or frighten the victim.	Coercive control is designed to make a victim isolated, confused, dependent upon their partner and obliged to follow their instructions and live their lives according to their partner's orders.
Grooming	Grooming is largely referred to in the context of an individual preparing a child or another for the purpose of their own sexual gratification. There is a natural symbiosis between the definitions of grooming and coercive control.	Grooming: • can take place online or face to face; • usually involves an enticement to meet up; • may include presents and praise; • means that secrecy will be demanded; • may involve threats of violence if the grooming acts are going to be revealed.
Immigrant status	Immigration status relates to an individual's legal status as a citizen of a country.	There is considerable dissatisfaction, particularly on the right wing of UK politics, against immigration. This leads to animosity and hate crimes being perpetrated against immigrants, often in the belief they are illegal.
Isolation	Isolation occurs particularly in many situations described. An individual becomes isolated away from family, friends or the authorities due to personal decisions or through the acts of a perpetrator.	A vulnerable individual may be an attractive proposition to a criminal if they identify them as isolated from any support systems.
Lack of power	A lack of power can feature in the lives of many vulnerable individuals. Vulnerability implies that an individual may not be autonomous in their decision-making due to mental health issues, physical or learning disabilities.	One of the main themes within the cycle of abuse is the lack of power as a victim. The theory sees the victim evolve into an offender where there is a sense of power which was lacking as a victim.

Table 3.3 *(continued)*

Extrinsic factor	Description	Comments
Lack of support	Vulnerable individuals may not have support mechanisms in place or may have purposely ignored them. A lack of support from social services, health and mental health services may then render the individual more vulnerable.	In most cases where tragedy has occurred due to vulnerability, a lack of support has been identified as one of the main factors, whether from the police, social services or another agency.
Language barriers	This could link with several other extrinsic factors. The inability to communicate clearly would be a considered factor, either due to English not being their first language or due to being mute or deaf.	The case study around Bijan Ebrahimi revealed that some police officers claimed and used the excuse that it was difficult to understand Bijan when dealing with his complaints.
Poverty	Poverty could be caused by many factors but could make an individual vulnerable to offers. Poverty is a growing phenomenon in the UK.	Adverse community environments can lead individuals into areas where negative consequences are more likely. Poverty is one such area.
Presence of an abuser	This links directly with the factors of coercive control and grooming.	In the area of domestic abuse particularly, the presence of the abuser, coupled with coercive control, isolation and a lack of power for the victim would make the victim extremely vulnerable.
Risky behaviour	An individual who places themselves in harm's way, perhaps intentionally but more like inadvertently.	The theory of victim precipitation discussed in Chapter 4 is relevant here. The victim can be a causal factor in becoming a victim, quite often through demonstrating risky behaviour. There is a need to be careful not to blame the victim.

The list of extrinsic factors in Table 3.3 is not exhaustive but illustrates the wide range of factors that may need to be considered.

CRITICAL THINKING ACTIVITY 3.3

LEVEL 5

Revisit the cases of Fiona Pilkington (Chapter 1) and Bijan Ebrahimi (this chapter).

- Make a list in each case of the personal factors that you can identify as relevant to that case.
- Using the information in Table 3.3, make a list of relevant extrinsic factors in both cases.
- Finally, create a list of any comparisons between the two cases.

Sample answers are provided at the end of this book.

EVIDENCE-BASED POLICING

In one area of policing vulnerability, a risk assessment tool has been devised to assess the incident in order to grade it in terms of seriousness and risk. The tool is the Domestic Abuse, Stalking and Honour-Based Violence (DASH) procedure. The DASH risk assessment (2009) has 27 standardised questions on it for the officer to ask the victim. (College of Policing, 2016b). (It is important to point out there are variations of DASH risk assessment which ask fewer questions.) As a result of the responses, the officer will record a risk assessment grading of either standard, medium or high. As a result of the grading (confirmed by a supervisor), there will be appropriate safeguarding measures put in place. Figure 3.2 lists the questions which need to be asked of the victim.

Q.1 Has the current incident resulted in injury?

Q.2 Are you very frightened?

Q.3 What are you afraid of? Is it further injury/violence?

Q.4 Do you feel isolated from friends/family?

Q.5 Are you depressed/having suicidal thoughts?

Q.6 Have you separated/tried to separate in the last year?

Q.7 Is there conflict over child contact?

Q.8 Do they constantly text/call/contact/follow/stalk/harass you?

Q.9 Are you currently pregnant or have you had a baby in the past 18 months?

Q.10 Are there any children/stepchildren not belonging to the abuser, or other dependants, in the household?

Q.11 Have they ever hurt the children/dependants?

Q.12 Have they ever threatened to hurt/kill children/dependants?

Q.13 Is abuse happening more often?

Q.14 Is abuse getting worse?

Q.15 Do they try to control everything you do or are they excessively jealous?

Q.16 Have they ever used weapons/objects to hurt you?

Q.17 Have they ever threatened to kill you/someone else, and you believed them?

Q.18 Have they ever attempted to strangle/choke/suffocate/drown you?

Q.19 Do they do/say things of a sexual nature that make you feel bad or that physically hurt you or someone else?

Q.20 Is there another person who has threatened you or that you are afraid of?

Q.21 Do you know if they have hurt anyone else?

Q.22 Have they ever mistreated an animal or the family pet?

Q.23 Are there financial issues? For example, are you dependent on them for money/have they recently lost their job?

Q.24 Have there been problems in past year with drugs/alcohol/mental health leading to problems in leading a normal life?

Q.25 Have they ever threatened/attempted suicide?

Q.26 Have they ever breached bail/injunction/other agreement for when they can see you/the children?

Q.27 Do you know if they have ever been in trouble with the police/have a criminal history?

Figure 3.2 The DASH questions (College of Policing, 2016b)

Table 3.4 provides an overview of the various risk levels that an officer can select, depending upon the information.

Table 3.4 DASH risk levels

DASH risk categories	Comment
Standard	The evidence obtained does not indicate the likelihood of the perpetrator causing serious harm to the victim.
Medium	The questions asked have revealed recognisable indicators of the risk of serious harm. The perpetrator has potential to cause serious harm to the victim but is unlikely to do so unless there is a change in their circumstances. A change such as failure to take medication, a relationship breakdown, or drug/alcohol misuse.
High	There are clear indicators that the perpetrator creates a risk of serious harm. The potential risk could happen at any time and the impact would be serious.

WHAT IS THE PURPOSE OF THE DASH ASSESSMENT?

For the police officer recording the DASH with the victim there are several purposes that the assessment satisfies.

- A thorough risk assessment will ultimately save lives and allow early identification of risk and incisive interventions which will prevent any future harm or risk of harm.
- It will clearly identify any subsequent needs of the victim, and will allow effective information sharing with partner agencies and charitable organisations working with victims of DASH offences.
- It will underpin an effective police investigation and will allow appropriate decision-making.
- The assessment creates a common understanding across agencies to refer an individual case to the appropriate risk management meeting such as multi-agency risk assessment conference (MARAC). MARAC will be discussed in the next chapter.

There are many academics and professionals who contemplate the DASH risk assessment and its actual benefits and advantages. It is clear, as one group of academics identify, that DASH was a:

> *landmark moment in the development in risk assessment to domestic abuse.*
>
> (Turner et al, 2019, p 1028)

However, the DASH proforma must be continually examined and improved to ensure that vulnerable victims are afforded proper protection and safeguarding. Turner et al (2019) also found that quite often only high-risk cases attracted appropriate action and support. They also identified that DASH is not that successful in highlighting cases of revictimisation and recidivism. While DASH is only one aspect of a series of systems and protocols, the systematic failures of Avon and Somerset Police in the Ebrahimi case may indicate that there could be an element of chance that drilling down into the case of a vulnerable person may not always identify them to be a repeat victim and possibly fail to focus on the recidivist actions of the perpetrator.

HOW DO INTRINSIC AND EXTRINSIC FACTORS COMBINE TO INCREASE THE RISK OF HARM?

In Critical thinking activity 3.3, you considered and identified the personal factors that could be determined in the cases of Pilkington and Ebrahimi. This was extended to consider where extrinsic factors were also impacting the issue. Another case study is examined to consider how combined factors can increase the ultimate risk.

Alice Ruggles was murdered by her estranged boyfriend in 2016. Alice had begun a relationship with Trimaan 'Harry' Dhillon in October 2015. Dhillon was a serving soldier during the relationship which started online while he was serving in Afghanistan. Their relationship was described as intense and unhealthy due to his behaviour; this led to Alice ending the relationship in August 2016. Dhillon then proceeded to stalk Alice, frightening her with his behaviour, which included driving from his army base in Edinburgh to her address to leave flowers and chocolates. Alice complained to the police and Dhillon was issued with a Public Information (Harassment) Notice (PIN) (sometimes referred to as a harassment warning notice) which demanded he desisted the '*stalking and harassing*' behaviour. On 12 October 2016, Dhillon broke into Alice's flat and savagely murdered her. More information about Alice's case can be found at www.alicerugglestrust.org.

INTRINSIC AND EXTRINSIC FACTORS WHICH CONTRIBUTED TO ALICE'S VULNERABILITY

There are several factors previously described in Tables 3.1 and 3.3 which can be identified.

Table 3.5 Intrinsic and extrinsic factors: Alice Ruggles case

Intrinsic factors	Age – 24 years old
	Gender – female
Extrinsic factors	Adverse cultural influence
	Coercive control
	Grooming
	Lack of support
	Presence of an abuser
	Use of social media
Increased risk	Alice was vulnerable as a result of each of the factors listed above. While separately many of the factors would not have made her vulnerable per se, when combined they meant that without meaningful intervention and protection, she was more than likely to face a negative outcome at the hands of the perpetrator.

Alice was a young female living alone. She was 24 years old at the time of her death at the hands of Dhillon. These are clear intrinsic factors which, when considered individually, and perhaps even together, would not have identified Alice as vulnerable. In terms of the extrinsic factors there are more to be considered. She was clearly groomed by Dhillon in the early stages of their relationship; this became coercive and controlling behaviour quite quickly. Alice sought support from the police, and from the Army, but it was ineffective and failed to provide the necessary support to Alice. The Domestic Homicide review (a review between partner agencies to determine whether in the circumstances could things have been done differently) considered cultural factors, such as the fact that Dhillon was a Sikh and so honour-based violence became a factor which was recognised and considered as possibly relevant. One extrinsic factor, which is not previously discussed, concerned the use of social media by Dhillon to keep track of Alice and to facilitate their relationship at first, and later as a vehicle for the abuse. Dhillon's presence as an abuser, through his stalking and harassing behaviour, was the ultimate extrinsic factor.

As described in Table 3.5, Alice was at increased risk because of the combination of all the relevant intrinsic and extrinsic factors. While the police took certain action and the Army hierarchy spoke to Dhillon, these interventions were ineffective in terms of preventing the continued harassment of Alice and her ultimate death.

Table 3.6 Timeline, intrinsic and extrinsic factors and increase of risk – case of Alice Ruggles

Date	Intrinsic/ extrinsic factor(s)	Level of risk – increase or decrease
Early 2016	Grooming Gender Age	No reports to police. The risk level is low at this point (DASH – standard).
April 2016	Presence of abuser Coercive and controlling behaviour Gender	Alice is seen to be withdrawn, losing weight, had stopped socialising and moved out of a house share. Dhillon obtains control of her Facebook by changing the password. Evidence of stalking and harassing behaviour. No reports to police. The risk level is rising as more extrinsic factors become involved and, if reported, may have attracted a DASH medium grading.
August/ September 2016	Coercive and controlling behaviour Presence of abuser Gender	The harassing behaviour of Dhillon increases, Alice is inundated with texts, emails, voicemails and is subject to emotional blackmail. No reports to police. The risk level continues to rise and if reported could have attracted a DASH medium grading at a minimum.
30 September 2016	Coercive and controlling behaviour Presence of abuser Lack of support Gender	Attended flat, rang doorbell and hid. Entered rear garden and left flowers and chocolates. Left message stating he did not intend to kill her. First report to police. DASH completed and deemed insufficient by Domestic Homicide review, but generated issue of a PIN. Northumbria Police considered his status as a soldier in Edinburgh to be a sufficient protective factor, ignoring his travelling history. The risk level should have been a high medium or just reaching a high risk standard.

→

Table 3.6 *(continued)*

Date	Intrinsic/ extrinsic factor(s)	Level of risk – increase or decrease
7 October 2016	Coercive and controlling behaviour	Parcel received by Alice from Dhillon.
		Recontacted Northumbria Police, no action taken.
	Presence of abuser	Breach of PIN, evidence of harassment offence.
	Lack of support	The risk level again should have increased, and now the DASH should have been high risk.
	Gender	
12 October 2016	Presence of abuser	Alice was murdered by Dhillon in the bathroom of her flat.
	Gender	

At key points the benefit of professional curiosity (as outlined in Chapter 1) could have led officers to link elements of the timeline together, which would have demonstrated Alice's vulnerability and increased her DASH score to high risk with the safeguards and protections that this would have afforded. The second call from Alice to report the breach of the PIN, which, while it had no legal standing, did provide evidence of harassment against Dhillon for which a positive action arrest could have been made to support the high-risk DASH proforma.

A CRITICAL ANALYSIS

The case of Alice Ruggles in Tables 3.5 and 3.6 provides a starting point to critically analyse whether intrinsic and extrinsic factors can provide an indication of increased risk to vulnerable individuals. It needs to be reiterated that an individual could experience one or more intrinsic or extrinsic factors but that it would not make them vulnerable per se. Also, an individual may be vulnerable on a temporary basis as a result of experiencing one of the factors, but it may not render them vulnerable outside of that temporary time frame.

The case study of Alice Ruggles also allowed a timeline approach to assessing how both intrinsic and extrinsic factors impact the likelihood of increased risk of harm. This is crucial when critically analysing the impact of the factors as it determines when the increased risk should be first identified. Some may describe this as the benefit of hindsight, and in relation to the case studies used in this book, it is both certainly and unapologetically the case. But it is also learning the lessons from past cases where successful outcomes were not achieved.

As discussed previously, the College of Policing has prepared an approach to identifying and dealing with issues of vulnerability. It has used evidence-based practice borne out of lessons learnt and the pockets of best practice around the wider policing family to inform new approaches. The College of Policing termed this review process a '*call for practice*' (College of Policing, 2021c).

This call for practice was to obtain examples of leading and effective practice in the areas of:

- identifying individuals vulnerable to harm;
- learning which communication strategies work better than others;
- looking at safeguarding practices which enhance an individual's safety, particularly in cases of multiple victimisation.

REFLECTIVE PRACTICE 3.1

- Reflect on the recommendations from this call for practice and a simultaneous desktop review highlighted in Table 3.7 below.

Table 3.7 College of Policing '*Call for Practice*' review conclusions (adapted from the College of Policing, 2021c)

1	Lack of a consistent definition of vulnerability prevented any real development of policing in this area.
2	The use of the Vulnerability Assessment Framework (VAF) was found to be useful.
3	Some common assessment tools are in use – THRIVE, NDM and DASH – but with little real evaluation of their true values.
4	Identification of many physical factors as barriers and enablers when identifying risk. Factors such as physical issues, interpersonal skills, social conventions and perceptions.
5	Considerable evidence of short- and long-term methods to keep individuals safe.
6	Little evidence of debriefing and reflection on cases.
7	Inconsistent training provided with regards to vulnerability.

Many of these themes have been identified and discussed in this book so far, such as those in points 1–4 and 7. Others (5 and 6) will form part of the ongoing analysis of policing vulnerability issues and identifying harm and the risk of harm.

- How do your reflections enhance your future practice and understanding?

Another development from reviews such as this and the evolvement of police training was the consideration of the voice of the survivor. As part of their recommended ongoing training, police officers should receive the personal involvement of survivors to '*tell their stories*' to inform future policing practice.

SUMMARY OF KEY CONCEPTS

Having read this chapter you should be aware of the complexities that can impact on situations involving vulnerability. The key concepts considered were as follows:

- the intrinsic or personal factors which can impact on an individual's vulnerability;
- the extrinsic or situational and environmental factors which can impact on an individual's vulnerability;
- the impact where intrinsic and extrinsic factors combine to the likelihood of increased risk of harm;
- the likely negative and often tragic outcomes where intrinsic and extrinsic factors are not identified by professional curiosity during an investigation.

CHECK YOUR KNOWLEDGE

1. Name five intrinsic factors.
2. Name five extrinsic factors.
3. Explain the opportunities that were missed to identify vulnerability prior to the death of Bijan Ebrahimi.
4. How many questions are included in the current DASH questionnaire?
5. What are the three risk levels associated with a DASH risk assessment?

Sample answers are provided at the end of this book.

FURTHER READING

Alice Ruggles Trust (2022) [online] Available at: https://alicerugglestrust.org (accessed 9 February 2023). The Alice Ruggles Trust was created to raise awareness of stalking. Its aspiration is to publicise the pertinent legislation so that it will be used effectively to both safeguard victims and prosecute offenders.

www.college.police.uk/guidance/vulnerability-related-risks/introduction-vulnerability-related-risk
www.college.police.uk/article/identifying-vulnerability-new-guidelines-support-police

The two suggested sites provide considerable supportive material to enhance understanding in the aspects considered in this chapter.

CHAPTER 4
THEORIES AND CONCEPTS RELATING TO VICTIMOLOGY

LEARNING OBJECTIVES

AFTER READING THIS CHAPTER YOU WILL BE ABLE TO:

- **describe the concepts and theories of victimology and relate these to real life policing case studies;**
- **explain the importance of early life events and their links to polyvictimisation;**
- **summarise the strategies to prevent repeat victimisation;**
- **demonstrate a critical understanding of the cycle of abuse and its links to future perpetration.**

INTRODUCTION

Policing by its very nature will bring you, as a police officer, into regular contact with victims of crime, anti-social behaviour and others who need support due to their vulnerabilities. The whole nature of policing has changed drastically in the last 20–30 years particularly in the area of dealing with aspects of mental health, vulnerability and risk during investigations into criminal activity.

This chapter explores, using case studies and other reflective activities, how a person could become a victim in the first instance. It considers many concepts and theories to provide a supportive understanding to new police officers which allows an opportunity to critically analyse the issues of mental health, vulnerability and risk alongside the practicalities of a criminal investigation.

Consideration is given to four theories of victimology to provide a basis for developing the ideology of how an individual could become a victim. Other factors such as impact of early life events, consideration of adverse childhood experiences (ACE) and links to polyvictimisation are carefully unpicked.

Later this chapter reviews strategies and initiatives designed to protect victims and prevent repeat victimisation, and other schemes such as the Troubled Families initiative. Ultimately, the question of whether victims become perpetrators is examined through an analysis of the cycle of abuse theory.

This chapter guides you to an understanding how a person can become a victim of crime, it develops a capability to identify a person's susceptibility to crime or their risk of being a repeat victim. One of the key abilities for a new officer to develop is '*professional curiosity*' around how the crime occurred and the status of the victim. We build on this concept first discussed in Chapter 1.

CRITICAL THINKING ACTIVITY 4.1

LEVEL 5

- When a crime occurs, often there will be a victim of that crime. List the factors why you believe a person may be more likely to become a victim of crime.

Sample answers are provided at the end of this book.

THEORIES OF VICTIMOLOGY: WHAT DOES IT MEAN TO BECOME A VICTIM OF CRIME?

Victimology is a study of the victims of crime and the psychological effects as a result of their experience. It emerged as an area of study in 1947. Some common questions emerge when thinking about victims: is it a case of being in '*the wrong place at the wrong time*' or is there a '*type of person*' who attracts offenders to them?

In 1948 Von Hentig (Maguire et al, 2007) believed this simplistic mantra of '*wrong place, wrong time*' to be insufficient to account for why a person becomes a victim of crime. He proposed a '*dynamic interactionist approach to victim precipitation and victim proneness*' (Maguire et al, 2007, p 463). This is one reason accounting for why a person falls subject to a crime. There are four theories which hold some credibility to consider here, as we try to decide how a person becomes a victim.

VICTIM PRECIPITATION THEORY

While this is a term proposed by Von Hentig, the crux of the notion of victim precipitation is that the victim initiates the events which lead to their becoming a victim. For example, in a policing context this might be where police are called to a public house following a fight between two men. Upon arrival one of the men is on the floor with a minor facial injury. Police officers determine that the victim was heavily intoxicated and became aggressive towards another customer who responded by defending himself and punching the drunk male once, knocking him to the floor. Hence the victim '*precipitated*' or started the event. The theory recognises that victim involvement can be passive or active, but that they engage in events which lead to their victimisation. It needs to be clarified that, in recent times, particularly around offences relating to domestic abuse and sexual crime, this theory does receive criticism as being one which could be interpreted as '*victim blaming*'.

The next two theories are often considered similar in that they both see the victim as an '*attractive*' proposition to the offender. While they do have some commonalities, they also have some differences. This is considered throughout the chapter.

LIFESTYLE THEORY

The lifestyle theory sees the victim creating and increasing the risk and likelihood of becoming a victim of crime. An example of a lifestyle theory could be where an individual is intoxicated, inhibitions are lowered and vulnerability is increased to an attack by a predator taking advantage of the individual. In a policing context this is a situation which is often alleged during night-time economy activities in licensed premises. Actions such as '*walking alone in areas of poor or no lighting at night*' or '*drinking excessively*' are examples of risk factors.

ROUTINE ACTIVITY THEORY

The routine activity theory requires three factors to be in place for a crime to occur. Factor one is the victim or target, factor two is the offender and factor three is the location.

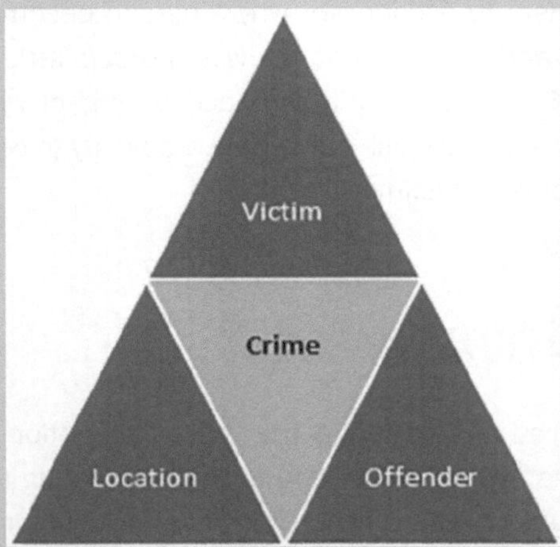

Figure 4.1 The three factors for crime to occur per the routine activity theory

When all three of these variables align, there is increased likelihood of an offence occurring and a victim being created. An example of a victim in the context of the routine activity theory would be an individual walking in a known area for robberies with their mobile phone in their hand, paying no attention to their surroundings and being unaware of the individual's intent to steal such items at that time and place. This routine activity theory will resonate with police officers who work around crime prevention and the problem analysis triangle (PAT).

DEVIANT PLACE THEORY

The final theory is referred to as deviant place theory. In essence, this theory considers that an individual who occupies a dangerous place is more likely to become a victim of crime. This theory clearly differs from the victim precipitation and lifestyle theories as the victim will often not have any active involvement in the impending crime. A policing example of this might be criminal damage caused to property on a housing estate which is suffering from congregations of youths in communal areas. The damage will be caused but often not directed at the individual who suffers it.

EVIDENCE-BASED POLICING

The College of Policing (2021d), through their *'what works'* evidence-based policing research processes, considers the issue of individuals who live in certain areas and suffer certain types of crime. Through collating research, both academic and from policing practice, it allows the development of evidence-based policing solutions to be shared. The discussion of the deviant place theory above has alluded to certain areas being targeted for crime for a variety of reasons. Research allows the police to identify where crime is occurring repeatedly and can be resolved through targeted police actions and activity such as proactive patrolling or targeting known offenders. If it sounds simple, it is, and can produce positive results. It can, however, create a displacement of crime from that area to another area for the duration of any proactive policing operation.

Understanding *'how'* a person may become a victim is important to the new police officer and links into other aspects of policing such as crime prevention. It also enhances an officer's ability to consider and identify where mental health and vulnerability exist and may increase the risk to the individual.

Look at this link, www.college.police.uk/research/what-works-policing-reduce-crime/people-and-places, and consider the thoughts of criminologists, police officers and others in relation to victims, places and offenders.

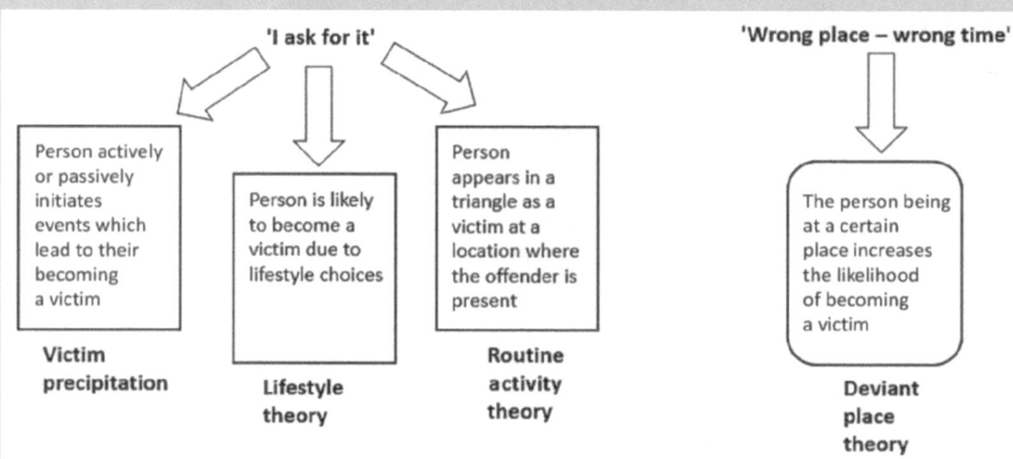

Figure 4.2 How do I become a victim of crime?

WHAT OTHER FACTORS CAUSE OR INFLUENCE AN INDIVIDUAL TO BECOME A VICTIM?

After considering the academic theories around victimology, it is important to reflect on what other factors could impact on an individual's actual vulnerability to becoming a victim. This section looks at the impact of early life events, such as adverse childhood experiences, the issue of polyvictimisation, the influence of multiple adversities, the idea of Stockholm syndrome and the concept of multivictimisation, or repeat victimisation as it is often referred to within policing.

WHAT ARE ADVERSE CHILDHOOD EXPERIENCES?

One of the more recognised concepts in policing today is the impact of early life events on the development of a person. Briefly discussed in the previous chapter as an extrinsic factor, these are more commonly referred to as ACEs. It is crucial for the police to have an increased sensitivity to vulnerability and risk. ACEs are early life events which can negatively affect the development of the child due to the trauma and stress caused by certain events. These events are documented to have immediate and longer-term impacts on both the health and well-being of the child and their life chances.

There are numerous ACEs, but it may be useful to categorise them as of direct or indirect impact. Table 4.1 lists some common examples of ACEs.

Table 4.1 Categories of ACEs (adapted from Ford et al, 2017)

	ACEs
Direct	Victim of physical, sexual or emotional abuse
Direct	Victim of physical or emotional neglect
Indirect	Witness to domestic abuse between parents/caregivers
Indirect	Experience of parental separation or divorce

It is accepted that the longer the experience, the greater the impact can be on the child, since the child's development will very much be influenced by their environment.

WHY IS THIS RELEVANT TO THE POLICE?

Policing is at the forefront of witnessing and experiencing these ACEs during routine calls and patrols. The police have a responsibility to observe with '*professional curiosity*' and if an intervention is not necessary or appropriate then to record and report their observations through the submission of a Public Protection Notification (PPN). Police reporting will aid local authority prevention opportunities, to both reduce and, in some cases, prevent ACEs from leading individuals into lives of crime and degradation.

Research has shown that individuals with experiences of four or more ACEs in comparison to individuals with no ACEs are more likely to experience and perpetrate criminality (Ford et al, 2017).

Table 4.2 Comparison: individuals with ACEs compared to those with none (adapted from Ford et al, 2017)

Comparison: individuals with four or more ACEs compared to those with no ACEs are:
14 times more likely to have been a victim of violence in the last 12 months
15 times more likely to have committed violence in the last 12 months
16 times more likely to have used crack cocaine or heroin
20 times more likely to have served a term of imprisonment

The relevance of ACEs will be considered again later in this chapter when we examine the cycle of abuse and the pathway of a victim becoming a perpetrator. This is certainly something which the comparison model above provides credence for.

POLICING SPOTLIGHT

On 3 August 2007 Baby P died, having been killed by his mother, her boyfriend and the lodger in Haringey. Baby P's injuries were horrendous, including a broken back.

There has been considerable information in the public domain about the failures of the police and other agencies in this matter; the formal Serious Case Review (SCR, 2009) report is a case in point. The full report can be viewed at British Association of Social Workers (2009). Some of the criticisms around the police are related to the apparent willingness to believe the mother's accounts without any serious challenge. One recommendation from the SCR for the police is related to their investigation process. There had been delays of over a week before photographs of the injuries were considered, which in terms of recording the best evidence is difficult to comprehend. The Metropolitan Police Authority report into Baby P (Bates, 2008) also noted the need to ensure all information during an investigation was accurately recorded.

→

The Laming report into the death of Victoria Climbié in 2000 (Victoria Climbie Report, 2003) is another example of where agencies have failed a child.

As a new police officer who may be involved in the early stages of cases like Baby P and Victoria Climbié, where police have been called to allegations of neglect or abuse, it is important to combine an open mind with professional curiosity. Look for signs of ACEs and apply your learning and understanding to the investigation. Use the national decision model (College of Policing, 2013a) to record your thought processes and decisions. This will provide you with a comprehensive and accurate record of your investigation, observations, conversations and decisions made at that time. Ultimately, if you are unsure, seek support from a supervisory officer.

WHAT IS POLYVICTIMISATION?

Polyvictimisation refers to an individual who is exposed to several different types of victimisation to a degree that the experience of victimisation is higher than that of the average person. Being a victim of different offences can be a demanding situation to be in, so it should be no surprise that victims have a reduction in emotional well-being and social functioning. This in turn leads to mental and physical health problems; children who '*suffer*' polyvictimisation can develop behavioural difficulties, which can follow them into adulthood.

Studies have shown how polyvictimisation impacts on children as victims. Findings have shown (Finkelhor et al, 2011, p 7) that certain pathways lead children into polyvictimisation. These pathways replicate what we know to be ACEs. This is another indication of the importance of police officers having professional curiosity when dealing with families and children.

WHAT DOES POLYVICTIMISATION MEAN FOR POLICE OFFICERS?

There are two considerations for police officers here to be aware of. Does a new police officer need to know concepts such as polyvictimisation? And from a practical policing point of view, is a victim actually a victim per se? The answer to those two questions (in my opinion) are – yes, police officers should be aware of the concept to investigate and signpost to the appropriate support mechanisms. In response to the second question – no, some victims have greater needs, and the indications are that these victims are likely to need greater support and understanding. This means the police officer should not '*treat all victims the same*'. Clearly, as a police officer with a knowledge of ACEs and identifying a victim as potentially a polyvictim there will be a need for an empathetic approach and a consideration of referral to partner agencies such as social services and mental health services through the reporting PPN system. Signposting to other agencies such as Victim Support should be actioned as required by force policies dealing with victims.

WHAT ARE MULTIPLE ADVERSITIES?

This concept considers when families face numerous adversities which can have a chain reaction and negative impact on the development and welfare of children. There are several adversities which can impact the family unit. Three of the main ones are:

- domestic abuse;
- substance abuse;
- mental health issues.

The reality for children is that, when faced with these multiple adversities, they can be left vulnerable to harm and sexual abuse (NSPCC, 2018). The more feasible impacts on children suffering from adversities (early life experiences) include mental health problems, poor performance at school, self-harm and suicidal thoughts, and problems with friendships and relationships.

The picture that the theories and concepts are painting is extremely pertinent for policing. It is easy to imagine how the pathways to becoming a victim are exacerbated by adverse childhood experiences, multiple adversities and polyvictimisation.

HOW IS STOCKHOLM SYNDROME RELEVANT TO VICTIMOLOGY?

Stockholm syndrome was a concept borne out of a failed robbery in Stockholm, Sweden, in 1973. During the robbery, several hostages were taken and held in a stand-off with the police. The concept is quite paradoxical; the victims (hostages) develop feelings of trust and affection towards their captor or kidnapper as a psychological bond that matures during the process of captivity. In the instance of the Stockholm robbery, this was illustrated through the fact that the hostages were hostile towards the police and refused to testify against their captor in court.

In one sense, Stockholm syndrome could be seen as a coping strategy, but there are four clear key points which can be identified (adapted from Jülich, 2005):

1 the victim or captive demonstrates positive feelings towards their captor, despite threats and isolation;

2. there has been no previous relationship between the victim/captive and the captor;

3. the victim subsequently fails to assist the authorities and often does not take any opportunity to escape;

4. the victim or captive does not recognise the captor as a threat and often identifies with the viewpoint of the captor.

How does this relate to the theories and concepts we have examined in relation to victimology? One main observation relates to child victims of sexual abuse. It could be considered that victims of sexual abuse may develop bonds with their abuser as were developed between the captive and captor. The paradox is that the very nature of sexual abuse should ensure that the victim makes a complaint about that criminal act, but in many cases they do not (Jülich, 2005). There are powerful comparisons to be drawn with serial sexual predators such as Jimmy Savile, whose offending, while not familial, went unchecked for years. This is sometimes considered to be a psychological issue where there is a link to power and authority over a vulnerable person/child (Namnyak et al, 2008). We will revisit this theme of power later in the chapter when we consider the cycle of abuse.

HOW DOES MULTIVICTIMISATION IMPACT VICTIMOLOGY?

Multivictimisation is a concept where a small percentage of victims suffer a larger than average percentage of crime. According to the British Crime Survey in 1982 and Farrell (1992), 70 per cent of incidents were reported by 14 per cent of all respondents.

There has long been consideration around the fact that there are a small group of recidivist offenders responsible for a disproportionate amount of crime, but the idea that there is a group of vulnerable individuals who are also at a disproportionate risk of crime has recently been receiving appropriate attention. This is a vital area for crime prevention approaches and for a joined-up approach from multi-agency partners. This is considered in more detail shortly.

The link to polyvictimisation is clear, as it is not one victim one crime type, rather it is one victim who becomes vulnerable to a variety of crime types. Why is this the case? Quite often the vulnerability of the victim is a key factor which attracts criminality and sees their details shared among the criminal fraternity, who would see them as an easy target. A current example from policing where a young person could experience polyvictimisation would be being used by a county lines gang. They could suffer assaults, sexual assaults, as well as be fully exposed to issues of child exploitation. Likewise, in the next chapter you will be considering young females who were repeatedly abused in Rotherham, which is a perfect example of multivictimisation.

Before examining strategies such as Operation Repeat (www.oprepeat.co.uk) to overcome the likelihood of a person becoming a repeat victim, a police officer can readily recognise circumstances where a person might become a victim through understanding the simple theories of victim precipitation, lifestyle, routine activity and deviant place theory. Certainly, in terms of an individual officer's crime prevention armoury, this would allow the officer to provide advice and guidance to prevent an individual from becoming a victim.

The officer also needs to be mindful of some other concepts and factors which can be as likely to increase the likelihood of an individual either becoming a victim or becoming a perpetrator. Awareness of adverse childhood experiences, other early life events and multiple adversities provide an opportunity to engage with partner agencies to offer the appropriate support. Similarly, being able to recognise the possibilities of polyvictimisation and multivictimisation also provide opportunities to intervene in the cycle of offending against vulnerable and young victims.

As a new officer, professional curiosity when dealing with a vulnerable child or individual could provide an opportunity to identify and support a victim who may be suffering from Stockholm syndrome.

CRITICAL THINKING ACTIVITY 4.2

LEVEL 4

- What can the police do to assist in instances of adverse childhood experiences (ACEs)?

Sample answers are provided at the end of this book.

STRATEGIES TO PREVENT VICTIMISATION

As we have discovered through looking at various theories and concepts of victimisation, there are several initiatives and strategies that have evolved to try and prevent an individual from becoming a victim or a repeat victim.

As a new police officer, one of your key taskings will be to prevent or reduce crime, and you will be tasked with upholding the Chief Constable's and the Police and Crime Commissioner's force aims and objectives. Another will be in the form of briefings to officers, where information and intelligence will be provided to focus proactive patrol opportunities to deter criminals and to catch criminals committing crimes in '*hot spot*' areas.

TROUBLED FAMILIES INITIATIVE (TFI)

Considering the impact of adverse childhood experiences or early life events and the issue of multiple adversities, what practical impact can you as a new officer have on these situations? A good example of police involvement with the initiative can be seen in Avon and Somerset Police's actions around their Think Family Early Intervention (TFEI) programme. This intervention was a force-wide response to the Troubled Families programme. They coordinated a multi-agency approach, providing holistic support for families.

> *Police community support officers (PCSOs) work with families to understand their key difficulties and identify what can be done to support them. The scheme has a preventative approach and aims to target low level problems before they become severe and high risk.*
>
> (College of Policing, 2021e)

Avon and Somerset's initiative was influenced by the TFI, which recognises that these problems need a multi-agency response and that the police are one part of the solution.

The government's TFI aims to support families and conduct interventions where they are experiencing multiple issues and problems such as crime, anti-social behaviour, truancy, unemployment, domestic abuse and mental health problems. David Cameron, Prime Minister at the time of the launch of this initiative, saw it as supporting parents taking responsibility for their children.

There are several observations which are worthy of consideration here. The TFI was aimed at parents of family units, seeking to make them responsible for their children. One observation relates to the starting point being the traditional viewpoint of what a family unit is. This has often been raised as a very '*middle class*' interpretation of what a family unit should be rather than the reality of what a family unit can be, such as single parent families (Boddy et al, 2016). Another criticism of the initiative is that a policy which seeks results is likely to be results driven. Would the funding be spent on families where a successful outcome was likely, rather than the more challenging and unstable family units?

The TFI was a multi-agency approach where it was accepted that the issues faced by many troubled families were not the remit of one sole agency. The initiative could involve numerous agencies such as housing, education, health, mental health, policing and the criminal justice system. As a police officer you may visit the same family household on numerous occasions to speak with parents about the low-level offending or nuisance being caused by their children. Quite often this is a reality for most response and patrol officers. It is also an area where youth offending teams become involved. What we have determined so far in this chapter would be that there are complex reasons in the background which need to be considered and evaluated as part of the problem before a solution can be reached. That first visit as a police officer to Mrs Smith about her rowdy and unruly ten-year-old son is the first opportunity to consider whether adverse childhood experiences may be a key factor here. If they are a factor, have they been reported? This is the professional curiosity that a new police officer needs to develop, as has been discussed.

Since the commencement of the initiative in 2011, it has received £1.533 billion in funding.

> *The programme supported over 400,000 families to achieve positive outcomes between 2015–2021. Each one of these outcomes means a family's life changed for the better, whether it has meant improving a child's school attendance, so they get the best start in life, supporting a parent to overcome their substance misuse and keep their family together, or supporting victims of domestic abuse so they can build a more positive future for themselves and their family.*
>
> (Loft et al, 2020)

Statistics that the government championed between 2015 and 2018 claimed the following results specific to policing and the criminal justice system.

- Adults receiving custodial sentences fell from 1.6 per cent to 1.2 per cent (25 per cent decrease).
- Juveniles receiving custodial sentences fell from 0.8 per cent to 0.5 per cent (38 per cent decrease).

These figures must be taken in the context of being compared to families with similar characteristics who have not been on the initiative. The context of this achievement is highlighted against what the report described as '*high-cost*' statutory interventions (GOV.UK, 2021).

MULTI-AGENCY WORKING GROUPS

While the success and value for money of the TFI can be debated, what is clear is that it highlights the importance of, and value of, multi-agency approaches to problems around victimisation. Within the policing '*book of acronyms*' there are numerous multi-agency groups which work together to resolve and support matters around such victimisation. Acronyms such as Multi-Agency Child Exploitation (MACE), Multi-Agency Risk Assessment Conferences (MARAC) and Multi-Agency Public Protection Arrangements (MAPPA) will become familiar to new police officers.

MULTI-AGENCY CHILD EXPLOITATION (MACE)

This is a strategic planning group with a focus on partnership activity to address issues of child sexual and criminal exploitation. This group considers the impact of '*county lines*' and the issue of missing children, and can be made up of the following agencies: police, children's services, health, education, housing, substance misuse, voluntary organisations and youth offending teams/youth services. This multi-agency group can make '*holistic*' decisions which support children using the relevant agencies for each case.

MULTI-AGENCY RISK ASSESSMENT CONFERENCES (MARAC)

This is a partnership working group to support victims of domestic abuse, particularly those at high risk of harm. Members of the group include police, probation, health, child protection, housing agencies, independent domestic violence providers and other statutory and voluntary specialists. The primary focus of the conference is safeguarding the victim of domestic abuse and frequently their children.

MULTI-AGENCY PUBLIC PROTECTION ARRANGEMENTS (MAPPA)

MAPPA was established in the Criminal Justice Act 2003 and is a regime which is in place primarily to ensure that violent and sexual offenders are managed robustly to ensure the safety of communities. The main agencies involved include the police, probation, prison service and Youth Justice Board. MAPPA therefore provides a coordinated opportunity for multi-agency working to ensure a holistic solution is applied to each case.

As a new police officer it is unlikely you will be involved directly with multi-agency working arrangements such as MACE, MARAC and MAPPA, but through the nature of your role you could be either supplying information or intelligence which will be discussed as part of those partnership arrangements, or you may be enacting a requirement which has been decided at one of the meetings.

REFLECTIVE PRACTICE 4.1

Each police service has different processes and protocols in place with partners. Conduct research into how your police service interacts with MACE, MARAC and MAPPA. Compare this by researching another force and consider the differences and similarities in their approaches.

- Reflect on and explain the positive aspects of these processes and protocols for establishing personal best practice.

POLICING SPOTLIGHT

Lincolnshire Police work closely with partner agencies within the MACE structure. Locally, there is a partnership information report under Operation Insignia. This report is utilised to submit information and intelligence by those agencies to MACE, thereby assisting any police investigation.

Examples of the types of information which may be submitted include the following:

- any sightings of any children or vulnerable adults with any '*high risk*' individuals;
- any places visited by those who are at risk, especially places linked with criminality;
- any vehicles that appear suspicious, which children hang around or get in;
- any telephone numbers used by high-risk individuals;
- any disclosures from vulnerable persons.

While as a professional police officer you will recognise the importance of the above types of information to an investigation, they should also inspire your professional curiosity when out on patrol and you see a vulnerable child who may be at risk from the county lines types of activities, to stop, observe and engage, but ultimately report the information.

OTHER STRATEGIES

One strategy which was developed as a result of elderly and vulnerable persons being targeted by criminals is that of **Operation Repeat**. This initiative is to:

Reinforce

Elderly

Persons'

Education

At all

Times

It is a simple method of assisting all agencies that are involved with the elderly and the vulnerable to ensure that they do not fall victims of crime in the first instance, but if they do to assist them not to become repeat victims.

Operation Repeat concentrates on criminal traders, bogus officials, doorstep crime, '*Nottingham knockers*', scams and email scams. It was derived in South Lincolnshire in 2001 when officers visited individual victims who had been targeted by doorstep criminals. Officers got to know the individuals and became trusted, which allowed them to feed into the conversation how these opportunist criminals worked, and make suggestions as to how to avoid being deceived by them.

As part of Operation Repeat, following publicity around the initiative, several mock doorstep scams were trialled. None of the scams were engaged with, nor were any details or money provided to the '*test*' criminals. Following this early success, the initiative was not fully developed until 2012 when it was granted funding and rolled out to the rest of the county. Subsequently, it has been adopted throughout the country. Importantly, and in keeping with the theme of multi-agency approaches, training was delivered to health care practitioners and social care workers. Thus, this supportive strategy to reduce victimisation and in particular repeat victimisation is now widely available across the country.

EVIDENCE-BASED POLICING

Operation Repeat is an initiative borne out of a police concept originating in 2001 where action was needed to protect vulnerable people from becoming victims of repeat offenders. The initiative grew from one based in the south of Lincolnshire to one which is now national. It now involves far more agencies than the police, and its purpose is to educate the vulnerable – in the case of the initiative, the elderly – as to the methodologies of criminals who would prey on an easy to target section of the community.

Doorstep crime is one of the areas that Operation Repeat concentrates on. One such phenomenon is that of the Nottingham Knockers. With goods originating from a warehouse in Clifton, Nottingham, these criminals knock on doors to sell their cheap wares at inflated costs. They also use this as an opportunity to identify vulnerable persons and targets they can either revisit or pass details to other criminals – a verbal version of the *'suckers list'* referred to in Jessica's story.

As new police officers, it is highly recommended that you visit the Operation Repeat website and read *'Jessica's story'*. It is an example of how individuals can be targeted and the impact that this type of crime can have on the individual and their family (Operation Repeat, 2022).

VICTIMISATION AND THE LINKS TO BECOMING FUTURE PERPETRATORS

Victimisation is, unfortunately, sometimes not the end point of the story. In certain crime types, such as child sexual abuse, it appears that on *'occasions'* being a victim can lead to that individual becoming an offender or perpetrator of the very crime that they were victim of. There is a school of thought among some scholars and psychologists such as Plummer and Cossins (2018) that being a victim of child sexual abuse is a major factor in the evolvement of the victim to an offender. While others disagree, Newburn and Stanko (1994) discuss the idea that some individuals are both victims and offenders. Research conducted by Plummer and Cossins (2018) analysed a variety of factors such as age at the start of the abuse, duration over which the abuse occurred, gender of the abuser, relationship between victim and abuser, types of grooming activity experienced, the type and seriousness of the abuse and whether the abuse was disclosed. This study was interesting in that their analysis identified evidence which supported the

> *existence of a cycle of abuse for male child sexual abuse victims who had experienced particular abuse characteristics.*
>
> (Plummer and Cossins, 2018, p 286)

One of the findings of research into child sexual abuse is that while females are more likely to experience the abuse than boys, it is boys that are more likely to become perpetrators when they grow older.

This cycle of abuse for male victims, according to Plummer and Cossins, follows four factors which are connected to the boys' transition from victim to perpetrator as illustrated in Table 4.4. These factors share a common theme, representing the experience of power (abuser) and powerlessness (victim).

Table 4.3 Differences between male and female experiences of child sexual abuse (adapted from Plummer and Cossins, 2018)

Differences between male and female experiences of child sexual abuse	
Age when abuse started	Male and female ages when abuse started are comparable, being 9.9 years and 9.6 years. One difference is that where boys were older when first abused there was a correlation with the development of later sexual behaviours.
Duration and frequency of abuse	Research revealed female victims were likely to experience a longer duration of abuse. There was no association with an increased likelihood of becoming an offender.
Gender of the abuser	Most child sex offenders are male, but research found that when women do commit child sexual abuse, they are more likely to abuse boys. Again, there is no correlation with becoming an offender.
Relationship between abuser and victim	While most victims of child sexual abuse are abused by someone known to them, girls are more likely than boys to be abused by a family member, parent or older relative. Some research suggests that there is a correlation between being a victim of a family member and becoming an abuser later in life.
Type and severity of abuse	Penetrative abuse is more traumatic for boys and girls. Girls are far more likely to experience penetrative abuse than boys. Research suggests that victims who experience more serious and invasive abuse are more likely to become child sex offenders.
Disclosure of abuse	This is an interesting area of research; girls are more likely to report the abuse and have the abuse substantiated. Boys who are abused by a father figure or peer often develop a '*relationship*' with the offender which may prevent disclosure. Some studies suggest that boys may be resistant to reporting male on male abuse for fear of being labelled homosexual. The normalisation of these sexual practices, which is described as a coping mechanism, is also linked with child sex offending when grown up.

Table 4.3 *(continued)*

Differences between male and female experiences of child sexual abuse	
Grooming methods	This is one area where it is believed that there is a correlation between the methods used by an offender to groom the child and becoming an offender in later life. One key difference between the grooming of boys and girls is that boys are more likely to experience force.

Table 4.4 Factors which may indicate a victim of child abuse is likely to become an offender (adapted from Plummer and Cossins, 2018)

Factor	Explanation
1	They were abused when they were 12 years or older.
2	They are subject to frequent sexual abuse which may become more severe.
3	They are subject to serious sexual abuse.
4	They have been abused by someone, such as a father figure, a person with whom they share a dependant relationship.

While as a new police officer this may be a difficult area to investigate and almost impossible to understand, it may well be that your professional curiosity identifies one of these factors in relation to a victim or a perpetrator and this can then be shared with the investigation team and other agencies that may be involved in the process, such as child services or adult services.

The concepts of power and powerlessness are worthy of consideration. The age of 12 should be seen as a key age in the development of a boy. It is the moment where personal development emerges and with it sexual identity. To be a victim at that crucial point must render the youngster subject to a state of confusion and a sense of powerlessness when faced with an older perpetrator, one who is familiar and who is respected, and will just increase the feeling of weakness and submissiveness at a time when the individual is seeking to demonstrate and assert themselves as a young person.

In the cycle of abuse, it appears a rational process that a victim who experienced such a sense of powerlessness, and normalised the sexual abuse, is more likely than not going to replicate those behaviours and actions as an adult, and as a perpetrator. In terms of the cycle, this would see power restored for the individual who now passes on the victim status.

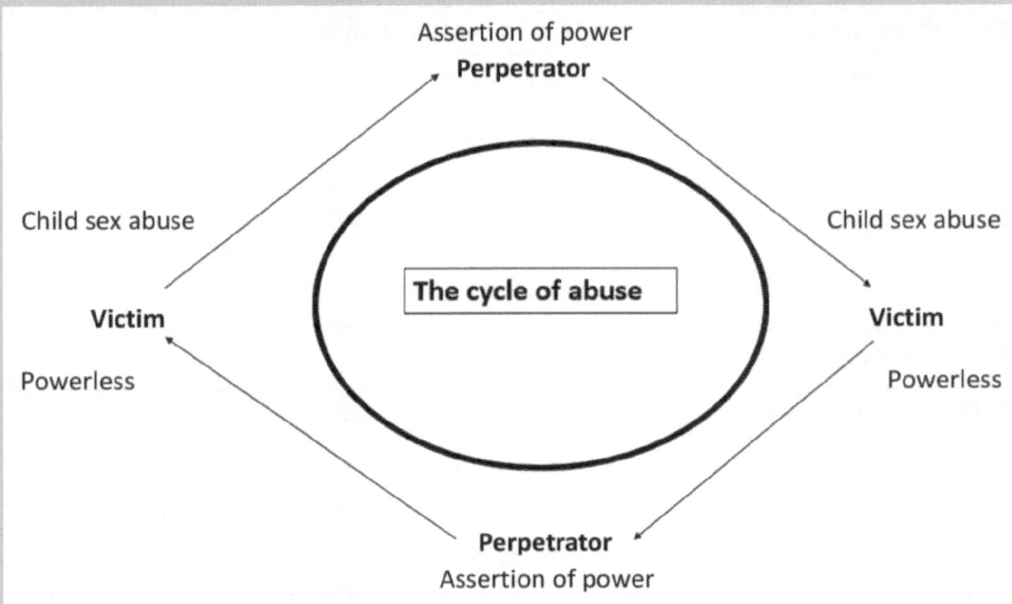

Figure 4.3 The cycle of abuse

The cycle of abuse is illustrated in Figure 4.3. The cycle commences when a perpetrator identifies a victim, in the context of our considerations, a young male family member, aged 12 or older. The perpetrator sexually abuses the child, rendering the victim powerless, while exerting dominance and power over them. Having been abused at a key age by a father figure, and the abuse may have been severe, when the victim grows into an adult, this abuse will have been normalised by the victim as a way of rationalising it. The victim may become a perpetrator, targeting a child with whom he has father status, and the cycle continues.

SUMMARY OF KEY CONCEPTS

The reasons why a person becomes a victim can be complex. This chapter has introduced you to some theories and concepts which will help you to begin to understand victimisation. The content will assist you in:

- explaining why an individual may become a victim;

- identifying the impact of early life events such as ACEs on a child's development and the negative impact when growing up, and the correlation with both offending and becoming a victim;
- interpreting strategies and initiatives which may be useful to prevent persons becoming a victim or repeat victim;
- recognising the cycle of abuse and how it can be used to possibly identify future perpetrators.

CHECK YOUR KNOWLEDGE

1. While on patrol you see a small male child aged around 11–12 crying in a park. You speak with the child, who appears confused and upset. You notice some small bruises on his arms and neck. At this point a male approaches who says he is the father of the boy. The boy seems pleased to see the man and calls him 'Dad'. What action would you take?

   i) Leave the child in the care of his father.

   ii) Speak to the father and ask about the bruises. Satisfied with the response, you take no further action.

   iii) Speak to the father, record evidence of the bruises, their locations and any conversation. Submit a Public Protection Notice with the details obtained.

   iv) Arrest the father immediately for common assault.

2. Outline the elements of the cycle of abuse.

3. Which multi-agency group meets to discuss issues specifically around child exploitation?

4. Why is knowledge of adverse childhood experiences important for a police officer?

Sample answers are provided at the end of this book.

FURTHER READING

www.college.police.uk/guidance/vulnerability-related-risks. The College of Policing web pages covering vulnerability and risk are a searchable resource around identifying vulnerability-related risk guidelines.

Davies, P, Francis, P and Greer, C (2017) *Victims, Crime & Society – An Introduction*. London: Sage Publishing. This provides a useful overview of victimisation and considers key issues in victimology.

Department for Communities and Local Government (DCLG) (2017) *Troubled Families Programme – Evaluation Overview Policy Report*. [online] Available at: https://assets.publishing.service.gov.uk/government/uploads/system/uploads/attachment_data/file/665504/Troubled_Families_-_Evaluation_Overview.pdf (accessed 9 February 2023). The report discusses in more detail the Troubled Families Initiative, examining the efforts that were being made to provide support in this key area.

CHAPTER 5
VULNERABILITY CHALLENGES FOR THE POLICE

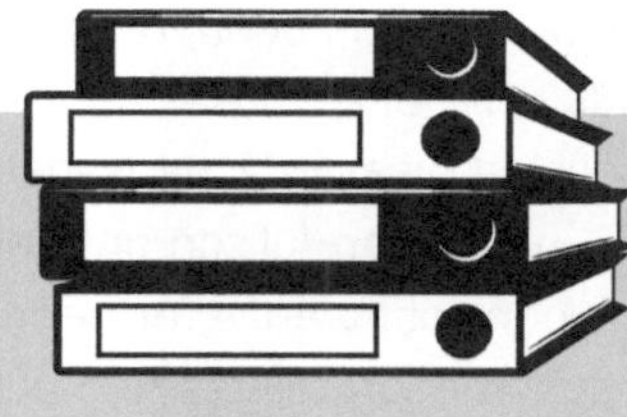

LEARNING OBJECTIVES

AFTER READING THIS CHAPTER YOU WILL BE ABLE TO:

- **describe incidences of child sexual exploitation and analyse police responses;**
- **explain incidences of online bullying and evaluate police responses;**
- **illustrate incidences of child exploitation and consider police responses;**
- **explain how county lines target and use vulnerable persons;**
- **discuss incidences of modern slavery and analyse police responses.**

INTRODUCTION

Modern policing is constantly being challenged and needs to be able to respond to these challenges. Many of the greatest tests faced by police in the last two decades have involved a vulnerability factor. Reflect on the College of Policing's definition of vulnerability:

> *a person is vulnerable if, as a result of their situation or circumstances, they are unable to take care of or protect themselves or others from harm or exploitation.*
>
> (College of Policing, 2021a)

This definition, although simple in its words, allows the understanding of how new crime trends and patterns are complicated for the police by the victimisation of vulnerable individuals. This chapter builds on the previous chapters and considers many new challenges and emerging crime types from recent times. Child exploitation (CE) has been mentioned already in this book, but the widespread and organised abuse of children and vulnerable adults requires closer consideration. The exploitation of children (CE) is another area where policing faces difficult issues. The emergence of county lines gangs, inextricably linked to CE, needs careful scrutiny and an examination of vulnerability and the risk of criminalisation of young children. A further area which one could be forgiven for believing was a totally new phenomenon relates to modern slavery. Modern slavery is a new phrase to identify a type of offending which has become extremely prevalent in the modern age. The reality of the centuries-old practice of uprooting individuals from their country of birth and taking them as slaves to a different country underpins the concepts of the modern understanding of these types of offences. The criminals who practice modern slavery and human trafficking target vulnerable individuals in order to maximise their profitable returns. Another area is online bullying, which has certainly become a very prevalent issue for individuals. While the issue of bullying is a much older concept, the instant access and mass availability of social media and the anonymity it provides means that the impact can be greater and have far-reaching consequences, particularly for vulnerable individuals.

WHAT ARE THE CHALLENGES FROM CHILD SEXUAL EXPLOITATION FOR POLICING?

In Chapter 2 the first real consideration of this issue, in this book, looked at the allegations which originated around the offending of Jimmy Savile and the subsequent and far-reaching Operation Yewtree (2011). In Chapter 3, the issues of CSE in Rotherham were introduced and the involvement of the National Crime Agency (NCA) under the banner Operation Stovewood was discussed.

CRITICAL THINKING ACTIVITY 5.1

LEVEL 5

- Write down your definition of CSE.
- Add a list of any CSE cases that you are aware of.

Sample answers are provided at the end of this book.

The starting point for a definition on CSE can be derived as follows:

> *Child sexual exploitation is a form of child sexual abuse. It occurs where an individual or group takes advantage of an imbalance of power to coerce, manipulate or deceive a child or young person under the age of 18 into sexual activity (a) in exchange for something the victim needs or wants, and/or (b) for the financial advantage or increased status of the perpetrator or facilitator. The victim may have been sexually exploited even if the sexual activity appears consensual. Child sexual exploitation does not always involve physical contact; it can also occur through the use of technology.*
>
> (Department for Education (DfE), 2017)

This is further clarified:

> *When a child or young person is exploited, they're given things, like gifts, drugs, money, status and affection, in exchange for performing sexual activities. Children and young people are often tricked into believing they're in a loving and consensual relationship. This is called grooming. They may trust their abuser and not understand that they're being abused.*
>
> (The Protect Project, 2021)

The College of Policing in their guidance documentation (College of Policing, 2021e) reiterates the definition above. It is a definition which is multifaceted. Table 5.1 breaks the definition down into easier to digest sections.

Table 5.1 What is child sexual exploitation?

CSE is a form of child sexual abuse with a child or young person under the age of 18			
Who by?	**How?**	**What?**	**Why?**
Individuals Groups	Imbalance of power Manipulation Deception In person Online	To generate and receive sexual activity	Victim – in exchange for something they need or want Perpetrator – for financial advantage or increased status
Grooming can make sexual activity appear consensual (CPS, 2021b)			

The definition caters for many of the cases that have been identified in this book. For example, Jimmy Savile, an individual perpetrator, using an imbalance of power over children and vulnerable adults, personally manipulated the victims into acts of sexual activity. The psychology and rationale of the '*why*' for both Jimmy Savile and in some cases for the victims is extremely complicated. There is no question Savile was a predatory perpetrator, but a few victims may have been enticed by the fame of the perpetrator, and Savile appeared to be comfortable in the media praise for his good deeds at the very hospitals and institutions where his offending took place. Savile thrived in the gaze of the media and public adoration. Truly an offender in plain sight. If Rotherham is considered, groups of perpetrators were involved in exploiting hundreds of young victims. A clear imbalance of power, mainly in person, involving manipulation and deception as well as intimidation and threats. The aim was clearly to obtain and generate sexual activity. The victims' stories occasionally feature in their involvement of being groomed obtaining something they desired, but for the perpetrators this was clearly for financial and personal gain at the expense of the victims (Jay, 2014). Review section 5 of the report where victim stories are discussed. The link for the report is available at: www.rotherham.gov.uk/downloads/file/279/independent-inquiry-into-child-sexual-exploitation-in-rotherham. Once you have reviewed section 5, move on to the reflective practice below.

REFLECTIVE PRACTICE 5.1

LEVEL 5

The College of Policing provides suggestions as to identifiable vulnerability risk factors that increase the likelihood of the child or young person becoming a victim of CSE.

- Review the College of Policing list of vulnerability factors: www.college.police.uk/app/major-investigation-and-public-protection/responding-child-sexual-exploitation/responding-child-sexual-exploitation
- Compare the risk factors identified by the College of Policing and link them to the victims' stories as reported in the Jay inquiry report.

Sample answers are provided at the end of this book.

There are numerous vulnerability risk factors which can be identified. The more common ones are listed below:

- the child or young person goes missing regularly;
- a member of a dysfunctional or chaotic family;
- a history of domestic abuse within the family unit;
- a history of abuse against the child including familial abuse;
- parents who misuse drugs or alcohol;
- the child suffers from mental ill health;
- the child has social or learning difficulties;
- the child has low self-esteem or self-confidence;
- the child is excluded from mainstream education;
- the child has active associations with gangs through relatives, peers or intimate relationships.

There is considerable overlap with the factors that were summarised as part of adverse childhood experiences in Chapter 4. The thread of professional curiosity again becomes important for the police officer when dealing with children, potentially regarding safety concerns or involvement in minor criminality.

CRITICAL THINKING ACTIVITY 5.2

LEVEL 6

As a professionally curious police officer who is investigating a call from a member of the public about a concern for the safety of a 13-year-old female, what warning signs might the female exhibit to cause you to consider a proactive policing intervention to safeguard them from vulnerability?

- List six warning signs that may concern you in their behaviour, attitude or demeanour.

Sample answers are provided at the end of this book.

The professionally curious officer should be triggered by many warning signs that a child might display. Some warning signs may need context against which they are considered, such as those associated with a change in temperament or personal physical changes such as losing weight or being malnourished.

REFLECTIVE PRACTICE 5.2

LEVEL 6

In the critical thinking activity 5.2, the professionally curious police officer recognised some warning signs that a child may be vulnerable and at risk of CSE. As part of the investigative approach that the officer should now be considering, they may ask the child questions to establish whether their concerns are valid and justified.

The child may not disclose any answers which could be evidential or benefit an intelligence submission.

- List six reasons that you consider a child that has displayed warning signs and may have been subject to CSE may not disclose that they are a victim.

Sample answers are provided at the end of this book.

A police officer will experience in all levels of investigation the reluctance of a victim to disclose evidence that would allow a proper investigation to be launched. There are some common themes that have been established and are listed below:

- fear of the perpetrator;
- loyalty to the perpetrator;
- not perceiving they are a victim;
- believing they are consenting or acting voluntarily;
- holding a negative view of the authorities, so less likely to report;
- fear of not being believed;
- shame and embarrassment;
- fear their sexuality will be questioned.

Some of the reasons can be attributed to the grooming that has occurred, such as believing they are consenting or that they do not perceive they are a victim. Reasons such as shame and fear would be replicated for many victims of non-CSE crimes. The interesting reason of loyalty to the perpetrator reminds us of the concept of Stockholm syndrome which was discussed in Chapter 4.

HOW RELEVANT IS REPEAT VICTIMISATION TO CSE VICTIMS?

Repeat victimisation was discussed in Chapter 4. As you consider the CSE offending in cases such as Rochdale, Rotherham and through the expansive Operation Yewtree and other CSE investigations, there is a clear picture of repeat victimisation. The survivors of Rotherham as described in the Jay report demonstrate being repeat victims, repeatedly abused. Why was this the case? There were countless missed opportunities during the Rotherham CSE offence period of 1997–2013 by the police and social services, but what other factors can be identified to evidence the reasons for repeat victimisation?

Table 5.2 Repeat victimisation reasons

Reason	Comments
Victim returns to perpetrator again and again	This demonstrates the power and strength of the grooming process of perpetrators, even allowing for the CSE being enacted against them, survivors' stories repeatedly reveal the strength of the established relationship with the perpetrator.
Fear of the perpetrator	This is often one reason why an individual may suffer repeated victimisation, the fear of refusing the perpetrator or the inability to report the activity. In the Rotherham CSE accounts, many survivors suffered both polyvictimisation and multivictimisation (see Chapter 4).
Needing money for addictions	Another reason for not escaping the offending cycle is that the perpetrators make vulnerable individuals dependent upon them. In the Rotherham investigation there is considerable reference to perpetrators providing alcohol to young girls.
Sense of loyalty and affection towards the perpetrator	In terms of analysing the horrendous offending against the Rotherham girls, it is perverse to see this as a reason why they became repeat victims. It clearly links into the concept of Stockholm syndrome, and again gives weight to the success of the grooming processes.

Table 5.2 provides some common reasons why repeat victimisation may occur. It is also clear that the impact of adverse childhood experiences is incredibly strong in the stories of the survivors. Chapter 4 provided an outline of the concept of Adverse Childhood Experiences (ACEs), but the backgrounds to the children in Rotherham becoming victims include multiple accounts of being in care, dysfunctional family settings and already being victims of abuse.

WHAT LEGISLATION AND PROTECTION CAN BE AFFORDED TO VICTIMS OF CSE?

While there are many tragic and unfortunate case studies where the police, social services and other agencies have failed victims of CSE in the past, it is important to look forward and consider what powers and options are available to police officers.

Looking at the definition of CSE, and considering the offending patterns identified in Rochdale, Rotherham and elsewhere, there are several pertinent pieces of legislation which can be utilised.

- **Section 14 Sexual Offences Act 2003** – Arranging or facilitating the commission of a child sex offence (under 16).
- **Section 15 Sexual Offences Act 2003** – Meeting a child following sexual grooming (under 16).

- **Section 47 Sexual Offences Act 2003** – Sexual exploitation of children.
- **Section 48 Sexual Offences Act 2003** – Causing or inciting sexual exploitation of a child.
- **Section 49 Sexual Offences Act 2003** – Controlling a child in relation to sexual exploitation.
- **Section 50 Sexual Offences Act 2003** – Arranging or facilitating the sexual exploitation of a child.

These offences can be considered in more detail at the following location: www.legislation.gov.uk/ukpga/2003/42/contents. There are also other relevant offences within the Sexual Offences Act 2003, such as rape of a child and many more child sex offences.

WHAT OTHER DISRUPTIVE LEGISLATIVE MEASURES ARE THERE?

The powers provided by the Sexual Offences Act 2003 are largely those which the police and the Crown Prosecution Service (CPS) can use in a reactive way to deal with perpetrators once offences have occurred. There are other, more proactive powers which the police can use, in response to their observations borne out of their professional curiosity. Table 5.3 considers several of the more common powers.

Table 5.3 Disruptive legislation for CSE

Disruptive measure	Location of legislation	Commentary
Police protection powers	Section 46 Children Act 1989	This power allows the police to take a child into police protection for a period of up to 72 hours in order to safeguard the child from immediate harm.
Child abduction warning notice	Section 2 Child Abduction Act 1984	This allows police to serve notice to a suspected perpetrator to prevent offences taking place against a child.
Sexual harm prevention order	Sections 103A to 103K Sexual Offences Act 2003	This is a court order which can be requested for an individual who is believed to be about to participate in activities which would cause sexual harm to another individual.
Sexual risk order	Sections 122A to 122K Sexual Offences Act 2003	This is a court order in respect of an individual who has perpetrated an '*act of a sexual nature*' and therefore poses a risk of harm to the public in the UK or children or vulnerable adults abroad.

POLICING SPOTLIGHT

The common disruptive methods outlined above are designed to protect and provide safeguarding to vulnerable individuals being preyed upon by perpetrators intent on committing CSE offences. Another useful power is provided by the Anti-Social Behaviour, Crime and Policing Act 2014. Sections 116–18 provide police with a crucial ability to investigate matters of CSE.

Under section 116 police can issue a notice which requires the owner, manager or proprietor of a relevant accommodation (hotel) to disclose information when intelligence has indicated the premises are '*being or have been used for the purpose of child sexual exploitation*'. The police, where they reasonably believe child sexual exploitation is taking place, can request the owner, manager or proprietor to provide information about their guests. This includes the name and address, and some other relevant information, for example, age.

Read more about hotel notices at www.college.police.uk/app/major-investigation-and-public-protection/responding-child-sexual-exploitation/responding-child-sexual-exploitation

Child sexual exploitation is clearly a very important area for the police – an area which sees perpetrators actively and repeatedly targeting the most vulnerable individuals within society. Another area where vulnerable victims are targeted, and which attracts considerable media coverage, is that of online bullying.

WHAT IS ONLINE BULLYING?

Online bullying is often referred to as cyber bullying and it is any form of bullying that occurs using any electronic media devices, such as computers and laptops, smartphones, tablets or gaming consoles. There is a strong correlation with face-to-face bullying for victims of online or cyber bullying, particularly for children.

The National Children's Bureau 2022 suggests that 80 per cent of individuals who reported being bullied in person experience online bullying.

CRITICAL THINKING ACTIVITY 5.3

LEVEL 4

As a police officer you are visiting an address to speak to a 13 year-old boy who claims to be the victim of online bullying and abuse. Your investigation will be informed by your professional curiosity; what types of online activity might you expect to be informed about by the victim?

- Identify four types of online activity the victim may have suffered.

Sample answers are provided at the end of this book.

There are several reasons why online bullying can differ from face-to-face bullying.

- The 24/7 nature of online activity means a victim can be contacted at any time.
- There is likelihood of a wider audience and bullying incidents can stay online and are difficult to remove, such as an unkind photograph.
- Opportunity for evidence collation – for example, the victim could take a screenshot to evidence bullying behaviour.
- Online with false accounts, there is a potential to hide your identity. This can make the incidents more sinister and worrying.

WHAT CHALLENGES DO THE POLICE EXPERIENCE WHEN DEALING WITH ALLEGATIONS OF ONLINE BULLYING?

One of the biggest challenges is the collection of evidence. Quite often bullying text and pictures can be removed from social media sites. This makes it difficult to prove a case against the perpetrator of the online abuse. Quite often perpetrators create anonymous accounts, and this again makes it difficult to identify the perpetrator. In terms of the power cycle, the abuser is really in control with the victim usually powerless to stop online abuse.

WHAT POLICE ACTIONS CAN BE TAKEN?

A police investigation will look to collect all available evidence alongside a statement from the victim. Further police actions could include:

- conducting a Domestic Abuse, Stalking and Harassment (DASH) risk assessment if appropriate; if not, using professional curiosity, identify any risk of harm for the vulnerable individual;
- advising the victim not to engage with the perpetrator;
- encouraging the victim to collate a diary of evidence of online abuse;
- encouraging the victim to take and keep screenshots of the abuse;
- considering possible offences of harassment against section 2 Harassment Act 1997 or section 1 Malicious Communications Act 1988;
- safeguarding the victim and signposting them to supportive organisations and ensure the Victims' Code is complied with;
- advising the victim to contact social media site administrators.

Social media sites are becoming the battleground for arguments around freedom of speech and slanderous online commentary made by mainly anonymous accounts. What this encourages is something which is known as a '*pile on*', where an individual can be slandered and criticised. This is akin to bullying and has serious consequences. There are countless examples of where an individual has been attacked on social media and this has led to their suicide. Leanne Morrison is a case in point, a young mother who was being harassed and bullied online following the break up of a relationship (Cybersmile Foundation, 2022).

COUNTY LINES AND CHILD EXPLOITATION

Another area that needs to be considered concerns county lines gangs. This area is synonymous with child exploitation. So, what are county lines? A definition provided by the NCA is:

> *County Lines is where illegal drugs are transported from one area to another, often across police and local authority boundaries (although not exclusively), usually by children or vulnerable people who are coerced into it by gangs. The 'County Line' is the mobile phone line used to take the orders of drugs. Importing areas (areas where the drugs are taken to) are reporting increased levels of violence and weapons-related crimes as a result of this trend.*
>
> (NCA, 2018a)

The National Police Chiefs' Council (NPCC) published their definition of county lines in the Serious and Organised Crime strategy. County lines is a

> *term used to describe gangs and organised criminal networks involved in exporting illegal drugs into one or more importing areas [within the UK], using dedicated mobile phone lines or other form of 'deal line'. They are likely to exploit children and vulnerable adults to move [and store] the drugs and money and they will often use coercion, intimidation, violence (including sexual violence) and weapons.*
>
> (NCA, 2018a)

While there remains no legal definition of child criminal exploitation, it is considered to occur often without the child's understanding. Often, they are coerced and manipulated, although there is also an element of intimidation and threat in order to get the child victims to carry out the crime on behalf of and for the profit of others. Criminal networks including county lines groom the child victims by enticing them with promises of rewards such as instant wealth. The use of a third party, be it a vulnerable child or adult, puts space between the criminal gang and the police. The gangs modus operandi is explained as:

> *County lines crime relates to the supply of Class A drugs, primarily crack cocaine and heroin, from urban cities to market towns, coastal areas and rural locations by young people, using a branded mobile phone line.*
>
> (GOV.UK, 2018)

The other element where vulnerable individuals are exploited occurs in those market towns and coastal and rural areas. The gangs will often force vulnerable people from their homes or '*cuckoo*' them in order to establish bases for selling their drugs.

> *The county lines model involves modern slavery and exploitation of children alongside drugs supply and violent crime. The most recent national assessment of county lines, compiled by the NCA, suggests that there were more than 1000 lines in operation nationally with links to increasing levels of serious violence.*
>
> (GOV.UK, 2018)

More than 1000 networks or lines running class A drugs across the country certainly sounds like a crime epidemic. When the vulnerability of the young people, children and adults used by these gangs are factored in, the scale of the issue becomes apparent.

HOW DO GANGS TARGET VULNERABLE INDIVIDUALS?

The criminals are looking primarily for a vulnerable individual who is not known to the authorities, particularly the police and other law enforcement agencies. This type of individual is less likely to attract attention, nor are they going to be searched for if they disappear from their usual routines. The gang recruiters, however, '*fish*' in very '*fertile ponds*'.

There are thousands of vulnerable children and adults who have been subject to ACEs such as having lived in a setting where domestic violence is prevalent, living in poverty, having educational needs or learning disabilities, living in care or having substance misuse issues. These individuals will be groomed and enticed away from any support networks to work for the criminal gangs. The risk factors for these individuals are very similar to those already considered for CSE in Table 5.2. The recruiters will seek to exploit the vulnerable individuals not only through the grooming promises but by establishing a hold over the individual through establishing a debt, often referred to as '*debt bondage*', which needs to be repaid.

ARE THERE WARNING SIGNS WHICH COULD TRIGGER AN OFFICER'S PROFESSIONAL CURIOSITY?

In Table 5.4 below, the common warning signs as identified by individuals who have worked with vulnerable individuals who have been targeted and used by county lines gangs are considered and evaluated as to their viability as an indicator.

The common warning signs, while not exhaustive, can be considered as good indicators of possible involvement in a county lines crime syndicate. Some should spark the professional curiosity of the police officer engaged with the individual, such as possession of drugs and money and being away from their home area. When combined with others, the likelihood of the individual being involved in county lines grows significantly; possession of a '*burner phone*', new and unexplained injuries and peers with nicknames only would further add fuel to the flames of professional curiosity.

Table 5.4 Warning signs that may indicate child criminal exploitation (adapted from the College of Policing, 2023)

Common warning signs	Comment
In possession of drugs or cash, possibly plugged	An individual with no previous convictions or intelligence reports found in possession of drugs or cash is a real indication that they could be part of a county lines gang operation.
In possession of more than one phone, particularly a cheap mobile	A cheap mobile phone, which could be linked to the organised criminals and is often referred to as a burner phone and is disposable.

Table 5.4 (*continued*)

Common warning signs	Comment
Has travelled away from their home area	In a location with no obvious family links, evidence of travel from a city via train or coach services such as tickets should spark an officer's professional curiosity.
A change in their behaviour	While this could be a warning sign, it may not solely relate to being subject of child criminal exploitation (CCE), particularly in a developing child.
Has new and expensive possessions which they are struggling to justify possessing	An indication of grooming activity, new trainers, jewellery or designer clothing. Again, professional curiosity should generate further questions from the officer to the individual.
Unexplained injuries	New bruises or cuts could be an indication of force being used on an individual to intimidate them into performing criminal acts.
New friends or peers who use mainly nicknames	Association with individuals who appear to be known through nicknames and having no clear real personal connection, ie not close friends and having no local connections.

POLICING SPOTLIGHT

Analysis provided in an intelligence assessment by the NCA in 2019 indicates how vulnerable individuals are used by the county lines gangs. Both vulnerable males and females are targeted, although it appeared that male vulnerability was more openly exploited than female vulnerability. Females were likely to be sexually exploited for financial gain by the county lines gang organisers.

Table 5.5 considers the identified roles of the vulnerable individuals that find themselves involved in the county lines model of criminality.

Table 5.5 How vulnerable victims are used within the county lines crime model (adapted from NCA, 2019)

Activity undertaken	Analysis
Acting as runners	This is an activity which sees the vulnerable individual '*run*' or move the drugs from one location to another. This creates distance for the criminal gang from a very risky activity of transporting drugs.

Table 5.5 (*continued*)

Activity undertaken	Analysis
	The vulnerable individuals will often be required to '*plug*' the drugs. This involves secreting the drugs internally within the body to move them around the country. Depending upon where an individual may be stopped by the police there is a chance that they could have large amounts of drugs or large amounts of cash about their person. They are also likely to be in possession of a weapon.
Cutting or bagging the drugs	Some of the vulnerable individuals will be forced to assist with the preparation of the drugs into saleable commodities, through '*cutting*' the drugs, then '*bagging*' the quantity that will be sold.
Collecting debts	Some of the individuals will be tasked with collecting debts on behalf of the county lines gang. This activity is also very risky, and often leads to injury being caused to themselves or others. The criminals are again a step away if the activity is discovered by the police.
Commit minor criminal acts	As part of many county lines gang activities, the vulnerable individuals caught in the '*spider's web*' of criminality will be tasked to complete other minor acts of criminality such as shoplifting. This supplements the income of the gang.
Cuckooing premises	At the beginning of this type of venture, the vulnerable owner or occupier of the premises was the likely victim. As the county lines model evolved, quite often the runners and other vulnerable victims of this type of criminality would find themselves staying at a cuckooed premises. Here they would be unpaid, receive no food and no health care.
Engagement in sexual activity	While females also feature as runners and are involved in other aspects of the county lines model, they are more likely to be exploited sexually by the gangs for financial gain.

The benefit of this level of understanding assists the police and other law enforcement agencies when they come across situations where, using their professional curiosity, they can consider the bigger picture. An example of a routine police activity would be where an officer stops a young person aged 12 or 13 who was identified as having just stolen from a shop. To all intents and purposes, a simple shoplifting offence. During the search, which could be under section 1 or section 32 Police and Criminal Evidence Act (PACE) 1984, depending upon the circumstances, the officer finds a rail ticket from London to the market town where the offence took place. They find a cheap mobile phone, an amount of cash which the person cannot explain having. When asked for an address, they give an address known to the officer as sheltered accommodation for individuals with learning disabilities.

Without a knowledge of warning signs of CE and how the county lines crime model works, these things may not be connected and a '*bigger picture*' not recognised.

For more information relating to the NCA intelligence assessment into county lines, vulnerability and harm, consult: www.nationalcrimeagency.gov.uk/who-we-are/publications/257-county-lines-drug-supply-vulnerability-and-harm-2018/file

A report by His Majesty's Inspectorate of Constabulary and Fire & Rescue Services identified that

> *it would be better to track all the various ways in which people can be vulnerable in a comprehensive process rather than considering county lines vulnerability separately. This is because people can be vulnerable in many ways simultaneously (for example, a child in care may also have mental health problems) and can face many forms of exploitation and abuse – physical, emotional, financial or sexual.*
>
> (Justice Inspectorates, 2020)

EVIDENCE-BASED POLICING

RESPONSE TO THE THREAT OF COUNTY LINES

The National County Lines Coordination Centre was established in September 2018 and is a multi-agency team comprising law enforcement personnel such as members of the NCA, police and other regional crime organisations.

This development arose as part of the realisation of the impact county lines was having not only on the lives of some of the vulnerable members of society, but also as a result of it having established a very successful and lucrative criminal business model.

The National County Lines Coordination Centre brought together

> *officers from the NCA, police and regional organised crime units to develop the national intelligence picture, prioritise action against the most serious offenders, and engage with partners across government, including in the health, welfare and education spheres, to tackle the wider issues.*
>
> (NCA, 2018b)

The NCA claimed in 2019 that within its first year of operation it safeguarded over 1000 children from the exploitation of the county lines criminal structures. They put this success down to:

- developing the national intelligence picture in relation to these criminal networks and how they identify and utilise vulnerable individuals;
- proactively targeting county lines networks;
- maximising the engagement with partners from the sectors of health, welfare and education spheres to tackle wider issues.

MODERN SLAVERY

A further challenge to the police when both identifying and then supporting vulnerable individuals is in the area of modern slavery and human trafficking. There are several useful definitions which help in building a firm picture of what this phenomenon is. Modern slavery is very much an umbrella term which covers a whole host of activities.

Section 1 a & b of the Modern Slavery Act 2015 states that:

> *A person commits an offence if –*
>
> *(a) the person holds another person in slavery or servitude and the circumstances are such that the person knows or ought to know that the other person is held in slavery or servitude, or*
>
> *(b) the person requires another person to perform forced or compulsory labour and the circumstances are such that the person knows or ought to know that the other person is being required to perform forced or compulsory labour.*

The legislation provides some key terms to consider: slavery, servitude, and forced or compulsory labour. Section 2 of the Act introduces the phrase human trafficking, while section 3 provides a consideration of exploitation.

WHAT IS SLAVERY?

The term slavery has recently been back in the consciousness of British communities, largely borne out of recent Black Lives Matter protests. The College of Policing provided a definition of what slavery is for our purposes here:

> *Slavery is described as the status or condition of a person over whom any, or all, of the powers attaching the right of ownership are exercised.*
>
> (College of Policing, 2017)

There is an obvious correlation here between a modern definition and a historic one – the very fact that any individual can be owned and thereby bought and sold and used regardless of their actual rights.

WHAT IS SERVITUDE?

The concept of servitude, while clearly linked to that of slavery, is described as a '*particularly serious form of denial of freedom*'. It can include:

- an obligation to provide certain services to another;
- an obligation on the individual forced into servitude to live on the other's property;
- the removal of the individual's rights, which hinders their independent status and renders them effectively as an item of property rather than as an individual.

WHAT IS FORCED OR COMPULSORY LABOUR?

The implication is that an individual has no rights and cannot choose to work or not. They are forced to provide a service which can be by means of coercion, deception or threat. This is linked to the idea of a lack of freedom of choice and ownership.

WHAT IS HUMAN TRAFFICKING?

This is defined in section 2 (subsections 1 and 2) of the Modern Slavery Act 2015 as:

> *A person commits an offence if the person arranges or facilitates the travel of another person ('V') with a view to V being exploited.*
>
> *It is irrelevant whether V consents to the travel (whether V is an adult or a child).*

There are some interesting concepts for police officers to consider. It is a wide-ranging offence where an individual, the trafficker, could be involved in one small part of the actual offence which is the exploitation of an individual. Table 5.6 summarises the roles which can be undertaken for the purpose of exploitation of individuals.

Table 5.6 Human trafficking participating offending roles

Action / Role	Exploitation
Arranger – Recruiter – actively recruits individuals	Irrelevant whether the individual consents to travelling or not.
Arranger – Transporter – arranges to transport individuals to the desired destination Facilitator – Harbourer – ensures individuals are controlled and contained	Travel includes travelling from one country to another, the terms departing and arriving are pertinent. It also includes travelling within one country from one place to another.
Facilitator – Receiver – receives individuals following transportation Facilitator – Exchanger – hands over individuals to the purchasers of the individuals	The trafficking can be achieved through the threat of violence, coercion, fraud, deception, by actual payment or in any way to obtain the consent of the individual and to exert control over them.

There is a subtle difference between human trafficking as defined above and people smuggling that needs consideration. People smuggling is where criminal gangs accept payment to provide passage to individuals to illegally enter another sovereign state in breach of their immigration laws and controls. While also a criminal enterprise, people smuggling is clearly distinct from the purposes of human trafficking. There is symmetry around the fact that some of the people being smuggled are vulnerable individuals.

WHAT ARE THE MAIN TYPES OF MODERN SLAVERY?

The results of research in 2017 created a typology of the main incidences of modern slavery. The research looked at how law enforcement agencies viewed certain activities and how they identified whether offences had taken place. The results were the identification of 17 types of modern slavery which they placed within four main types or groupings.

Table 5.7 Main types of modern slavery (adapted from GOV.UK, 2017)

Offence types	Recruitment	Elements of control
Exploitation of labour	Various types of activities Vulnerable individuals approached	Use of violence, threat of violence, debt bondage, emotional stress or social isolation
Domestic servitude	Partner abuse, relative abuse or forced servitude with unknown individuals	Use of violence, emotional stress and social isolation

Table 5.7 *(continued)*

Offence types	Recruitment	Elements of control
Sexual exploitation	Group CSE, single CSE, forced sex work Considerable evidence of grooming of vulnerable individuals	Use of violence, use of substances to gain compliance and debt bondage, social isolation
Criminal exploitation	Gang activities, county lines illegal activities such as staffing cannabis farms Forced acquisitive crime such as shoplifting Forced begging	Use of violence, use of substances to gain compliance, social isolation

The golden thread of vulnerable victimology is crucially evident in the findings of the research. The activities perpetrated under the four categories have common themes. Many of the forced participants, the victims, are identifiable as vulnerable for one or more reasons. In terms of forced labour, often individuals are vulnerable due to their socio-economic situations, desperately needing work to survive, or coerced because of debt bondage. Domestic servitude is where there are close links to the vulnerability of partners within domestic abuse situations, as well as other individuals exploited due to vulnerability created by not speaking the language or being away from any support networks. Sexual exploitation fully exposes the manipulation of vulnerabilities of age and other situational circumstances by the perpetrators. Criminal exploitation, highlighted earlier in this chapter, also exposes how offenders are attracted to vulnerable victims.

The power of the offenders and perpetrators is enforced through common means: violence and the threat of violence, the use of substances and forced debt bondage, which is exacerbated by non-payment or limited payment for being involved in activities, isolation of the victim from their support networks and emotional stress which the perpetrators use to maintain compliance.

It is clear that offenders and perpetrators fully expose and use vulnerabilities to their advantage, often through powerful grooming activities, also enticing victims to enter a situation akin to Stockholm syndrome. When considered in the context of their vulnerability, this means that the police and other law enforcement agencies will need to use their professional curiosity and investigative abilities fully to both expose offences and identify victims in order to properly safeguard them.

CRITICAL THINKING ACTIVITY 5.4

LEVEL 6

You are on a routine foot patrol when a member of the public draws your attention to a distressed female sitting in a doorway of a block of flats. They express concerns about how malnourished she looks.

You speak to the female, and she is clearly upset and you see visible bruising on her arms and neck. You establish she is 15, speaks limited English and is from Bulgaria.

- Using your professional curiosity, how would you progress this encounter?

Sample answers are provided at the end of this book.

EVIDENCE-BASED POLICING

The National Referral Mechanism (NRM) (GOV.UK, 2022b) is a framework used to identify and refer potential victims of modern slavery. The NRM is intended to ensure victims receive appropriate support. Statutory organisations such as the police and many non-statutory ones have an obligation to refer a potential victim of modern slavery.

All individuals should be informed that their referral to the NRM will be passed on to the police as they are likely to be the victim of a crime. These referrals are either consensual with the agreement of the victim or, if non-consensual, through a third-party report to the police.

While the victim is under no obligation to cooperate with the police, if they do so, an investigation will be instigated following the recording of a crime. One of the first requirements will be to establish where the crime has taken place. If the offence has taken place overseas or it cannot be established which force area the incident took place in, it will be referred to the force area the victim currently lives in.

The Every Child Protected Against Trafficking (2020) provided the following analysis of matters brought to the attention of the NRM.

- A total of 4550 children were referred into the NRM.
- Children comprised nearly half of the total number of suspected trafficking victims in 2020.
- Of those referred into the NRM in 2019, the most common country of origin of these children was the UK (52 per cent), followed by Vietnam (9 per cent), Sudan (5 per cent), Albania (6 per cent), Eritrea (6 per cent), (no percentages provided for children from the following countries) Romania, Afghanistan, Iraq, Nigeria and Iran.
- Between April–June 2020, more children than adults were identified as potential victims of trafficking for the first time.
- In recent years there has been a particular increase in the number of UK national children who were identified as potential victims of criminal exploitation, sometimes referred to as '*county lines*'.

The NRM has proved to be a valuable repository for the recording of information concerning all aspects of modern slavery, but more importantly the ability to clearly identify vulnerability in the victims is vital to reinforce the need for policing and its partners to continue their work of supporting those vulnerable victims when identified.

STATUTORY DEFENCE TO AN ALLEGATION OF MODERN SLAVERY

There is a defence against an allegation of committing an offence of modern slavery. Section 45 (subsection 1) of the Modern Slavery Act 2015 states:

A person is not guilty of an offence if –

(a) the person is aged 18 or over when the person does the act which constitutes the offence,

(b) the person does that act because the person is compelled to do it,

(c) the compulsion is attributable to slavery or to relevant exploitation, and

(d) a reasonable person in the same situation as the person and having the person's relevant characteristics would have no realistic alternative to doing that act.

While section 45 (subsection 4) states:

> *A person is not guilty of an offence if –*
>
> *(a) the person is under the age of 18 when the person does the act which constitutes the offence,*
>
> *(b) the person does that act as a direct consequence of the person being, or having been, a victim of slavery or a victim of relevant exploitation, and*
>
> *(c) a reasonable person in the same situation as the person and having the person's relevant characteristics would do that act.*

Both elements provide a defence to an individual who is being investigated following an allegation of committing an offence under section 1 of the Modern Slavery Act 2015. This affords protection to those who have committed criminal acts as a result of being a victim of modern slavery.

SUMMARY OF KEY CONCEPTS

This chapter has examined some extremely key themes for modern policing. It has also identified how the criminals and perpetrators of these offences will target individuals with recognisable vulnerabilities in order to maximise the profit and gains from their criminal activities. The key concepts considered were:

- child sexual exploitation and how the police can recognise offences and responses that they can make;
- child exploitation, particularly considering the county lines model of offending;
- online bullying, the impact of the offence on individuals and the difficulty in investigating these matters;
- the wide arc of modern slavery offences and the policing response.

CHECK YOUR KNOWLEDGE

1. What is the College of Policing definition of vulnerability?
2. Name five CSE warning signs.
3. Explain the purpose of the National Referral Mechanism.
4. What is meant by the term cuckooing?
5. What is the definition of modern slavery?

Sample answers are provided at the end of this book.

FURTHER READING

www.college.police.uk/app/major-investigation-and-public-protection/responding-child-sexual-exploitation/responding-child-sexual-exploitation. The College of Policing guidance pages are a good repository of information with regards to responding to allegations of CSE.

Victim Safety and Support (2021) [online] Available at: www.college.police.uk/app/major-investigation-and-public-protection/domestic-abuse/victim-safety-and-support (accessed 9 February 2023). The guidance from the College of Policing is vital to inform the risk assessment and safety planning areas surrounding police involvement with victims of domestic abuse and is important reading for police officers involved in this policing context.

CHAPTER 6
RESPONSES OF THE POLICE TO IDENTIFYING VULNERABILITY

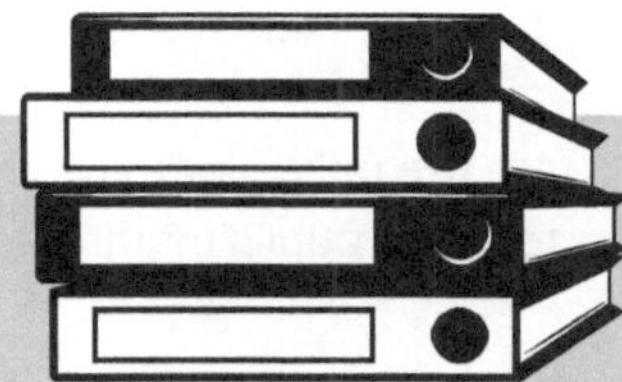

LEARNING OBJECTIVES

AFTER READING THIS CHAPTER YOU WILL BE ABLE TO:

- **describe how the police use risk assessment tools to identify vulnerability;**
- **explain how the police use certain protective factors and understand their limitations;**
- **discuss the complex landscape of vulnerability as a complicating factor in modern criminal activities;**
- **explain how police and partner agencies' responses have been driven by lessons learnt.**

INTRODUCTION

This chapter considers how the police respond to the risk of harm created towards the vulnerable individuals targeted by criminals. Crime creates victims. Certain types of crimes take advantage of individuals, sometimes as individual participants, and sometimes as one of a group of victims. Crimes such as those discussed in Chapter 5 – child sexual exploitation, child exploitation (county lines), online bullying and the various modern slavery offences – benefit from the involvement of the most vulnerable individuals in society.

The series of questions outlined below require attention to establish how effective the police are at responding to problems of vulnerability in victims.

- How do police officers and their partner agencies proactively identify individuals who are vulnerable?
- What mechanisms or tools are used to assist with recognising an individual who is vulnerable to criminals, and how the risk is reviewed and managed?
- What measures can the police use to prevent an individual from becoming a victim?
- Are the police learning lessons from identified failings highlighted in serious case reviews, public inquiries and other means of scrutiny?

HOW DO POLICE OFFICERS AND THEIR PARTNERS IDENTIFY VICTIMS OF CRIME WHO ARE VULNERABLE?

One of the aspirational policing intent statements is for policing to proactively identify vulnerable individuals who are at risk of harm (VKPP, 2023). In Chapter 2 the seven themes of the National Vulnerability Action Plan (NVAP) were considered and the themes listed below are pertinent here.

- Early intervention and prevention.
- Protect, support, safeguard and manage risk.

This early proactive approach ideally allows the police and partners to establish appropriate safeguarding measures to ensure the risk of harm due to the vulnerability is removed and eradicated. This proactive aspiration may be a reality now, but examining the historic policing of criminal areas where the individual had one or more vulnerability factors increasing the risk of harm made it clear that, at best, the police and partners were totally reactive.

Another important point when considering how the police previously identified vulnerable individuals is their continued improved performance against developing and emerging crime types, such as the consideration of the area of child sexual exploitation and an examination of the Oxford child sex abuse ring (1998–2012). It is possible to draw not just comparable historic points but also examine how such allegations may be dealt with today and so how much progress has been made in this area.

This activity also has numerous comparative points with the sex abuse scandals in Rochdale from 2003 to 2014 and Rotherham from 1997 to 2013. Table 6.1 considers comparable themes across the three locations.

Table 6.1 Commonality factors – Oxford, Rochdale and Rotherham CSE cases (adapted from Home Office, 2021)

Factor	Comment
CSE is under-reported	In each of the inquiries and serious case reviews the under-reporting of offences has been identified. This will clearly be linked to survivors' accounts of being dismissed by police and social services (Jay, 2014).
The main offenders are male	The main offenders were found to be male, aged around 30 years old.
Main offenders were from a similar ethnic background	In all three cases the main ethnic grouping of offenders were from a Pakistani background. Research has shown, however, that offenders who commit CSE are generally from diverse backgrounds.
Motivations of the offenders	• Financial gain • Sexual gratification • Misogyny • Disregard for women and girls • Sexual interest in children was not always a common factor
Grooming and enticement	• Contacts made locally • Parents and guardians persuaded of good intent of the offender • The victim believes they are in a legitimate relationship • Use of alcohol and drugs to reduce inhibitions and likelihood of reporting
Peer encouragement among perpetrators	There was evidence that male offenders encouraged and absolved each other in terms of involvement.

What Table 6.2 provides is summary analysis of the previously considered inquiries, reviews and overviews of the offences committed. Trends can be determined that will enhance the ability of the proactive and professionally curious police officer or social worker. For the professionally curious officer, because of being able to utilise past case studies in identifying the vulnerabilities of victims, it is possible to consider whether certain types of crime target individuals or groups of individuals. It is worth noting, however, that predictive strategies are not always successful, as with the Yorkshire Ripper and geographical profiling.

CRITICAL THINKING ACTIVITY 6.1

LEVEL 5

- Consider the offence types discussed in Chapter 5:
  - online bullying;
  - child exploitation (county lines);
  - child sexual exploitation;
  - modern slavery.
- Do you think that these offence types target individuals or groups of individuals? Write down a rationale for your answers.
- How did you decide whether certain offences correlate to targeting single victims or multiple victims?

Sample answers are provided at the end of this book.

Table 6.2 Offences and victims

Offences	Single victim	Multiple victims
Online bullying	This offence type is often targeted against an individual, often by multiple offenders.	It is unusual for this type of offending to target multiple victims.

Table 6.2 *(continued)*

Offences	Single victim	Multiple victims
Child exploitation (county lines)	County lines will target individuals in order to coerce them into the criminal network.	County lines requires the involvement of multiple patsies or innocent individuals to operate its criminal model.
Child sexual exploitation	CSE can target individual victims. Jimmy Savile is a case in point.	CSE can also target large groups of victims, as demonstrated by the grooming gangs of Rotherham.
Modern slavery	Many of the modern slavery offences are targeted against individual victims, such as those relating to domestic servitude.	Others such as CSE and CE can be perpetrated against multiple victims at the same time. Maximum profit against minimum risk.

Table 6.2 provides another prompt for the professionally curious officer when faced with a situation where, for example, a young female (14 years old) is found intoxicated in a local park in the presence of an older male (31 years old). There may be a plausible explanation offered, which a few decades ago may have satisfied the officer, particularly where the female appears to be comfortable and making no complaints. Now the officer needs to use their professionally curious mindset and investigate exactly what they have discovered. To that end they could use a form of risk assessment to establish any vulnerability and risk.

RISK ASSESSMENT TOOLS TO ASSIST A PROACTIVE INVESTIGATION

There are several risk assessment tools that could be used by the officer in the scenario above. As has been determined, an officer should use the national decision model (NDM) as referenced in Chapter 2 to formulate their investigation. The risk assessment tool will form part of the section of the NDM where information is being gathered. Risk assessment tools are often relevant to specific circumstances, but three main ones will be considered here, the THRIVE (Threat, Harm, Risk, Investigation, Vulnerability and Engagement) model, the VAF (Vulnerability Assessment Framework) and the DASH (Domestic Abuse, Stalking and Harassment) risk assessment.

CRITICAL THINKING ACTIVITY 6.2

LEVEL 4

Consider the contents of the earlier chapters in relation to the three risk assessment tools and refresh your knowledge of each: Chapter 1 – THRIVE, Chapter 2 – VAF and Chapter 3 – DASH. Focus on the circumstances of the young girl being found in a park with an older male.

- Write down your thoughts as to whether each of the risk assessment tools could be used in those circumstances.

Sample answers are provided at the end of this book.

THE THREAT, HARM, RISK, INVESTIGATION, VULNERABILITY AND ENGAGEMENT (THRIVE) MODEL

One tool used by the police to assess risk and vulnerability is the THRIVE model. As described in Chapter 1 the THRIVE model originated through work by the College of Policing in conjunction with a new definition of vulnerability. While the tool is used primarily to identify and prioritise which incidents require an appropriate and immediate policing response; it does assist in the example of the young girl with the older male. Through investigation, the vulnerability of the young girl should be established, the risk of harm as a result of that vulnerability will be identified as the threat, which through engagement and safeguarding can be removed and neutralised.

The three risk assessment tools considered are useful in particular circumstances to identify and measure vulnerability of an individual and therefore anticipate the risk of harm with a view to limiting the risk, protecting and safeguarding the vulnerable individual.

THE VULNERABILITY ASSESSMENT FRAMEWORK (VAF)

One assessment tool which may be useful in the above circumstances is the VAF model. As discussed in Chapter 2, during the gathering information and intelligence stage of the NDM the officer could incorporate the VAF. Using the ABCDE system the officer can start to interpret the scene before them in the park with the young girl and the older male.

- Appearance and atmosphere – The girl is intoxicated through drink, she appears considerably younger than the male, they appear not to be related and she is found in a local park alone with the male.

- Behaviour – The girl is drunk and is making no allegations. The male and girl were found sitting on a bench. The male appears uncomfortable at the police attention.

- Communication – The officer needs to ensure that the girl can be spoken to out of earshot of the male. Their accounts need to be taken separately and compared for disparities.

- Danger – The girl is intoxicated; she is considerably younger than the male. There is a risk of harm if she is left in that situation.

- Environment – A local park with few other occupants, only discovered by police by chance. This increases the risk to the girl.

The officer will now be assessing the situation, their observations, the responses to questions and, because of appropriate training, will be considering whether there are any warning signs that could indicate child sexual exploitation. In Chapter 5 several factors were identified which may be relevant in this situation. The officer can make further enquiries using the police national computer (PNC) and local intelligence systems into both the male and the young girl. This may assist answering questions such as the following.

- Has she gone missing in the past?

- Are there any domestic incidents at the young girl's home address on record?

- Is the young girl excluded from education?

- Is she noted as being involved in similar incidents in the past?

- Is the male known to the police?

- Does the male have any relevant offending history?

- Is there any intelligence on the male which may affect this situation?

Through conducting the VAF process the officer can determine a risk grading which may necessitate the officer taking action to safeguard the young girl.

THE DOMESTIC ABUSE, STALKING AND HARASSMENT (DASH) PROFORMA

The final main risk assessment tool which considers the vulnerability of the victim is the DASH risk assessment. The DASH questionnaire was highlighted in Chapter 3 and the standard 27-question approach was noted to inform a risk grading of standard, medium or high. The subsequent policing actions are dependent on the grading of risk and the resulting safeguarding measures. The DASH risk assessment was found to be a very substantial improvement on previous means of dealing with domestic violence, stalking and cases of harassment, but there are suggestions that, unless the risk was high, there were too many examples of insufficient protections being enacted. In terms of the young girl being in the park with an older male, the DASH approach appears unsuitable with the information that is available at that time. This has led to an initiative around Domestic Abuse Risk Assessment (DARA) where a different focus has led to questions to quantify, for example, how often abuse is happening on a sliding scale of never to all the time. DARA is a new risk assessment tool that has been piloted with considerable success (College of Policing, 2022a). It is an enhanced risk assessment which supports the police in spotting signs of coercive control and better supporting victims.

WHAT PROTECTIVE FACTORS CAN THE POLICE USE TO SAFEGUARD VULNERABLE INDIVIDUALS?

Once an individual such as the young girl above is highlighted as needing to be safeguarded because of the identified risk, there are several protective measures that could be used by the police and its partner agencies. A useful source of information can be found on the College of Policing website dedicated to investigating child abuse and safeguarding children (College of Policing, nd).

In Chapter 5, Table 5.3 identifies several legislative options for intervention and providing protection.

- Powers relating to police protection – section 46 of the Children Act 1989: www.legislation.gov.uk/ukpga/1989/41/section/46

- Child abduction warning notices – section 2 of the Child Abduction Act 1984: www.legislation.gov.uk/ukpga/1984/37/section/2

- Sexual harm prevention orders – sections 103A–103K of the Sexual Offences Act 2003: www.legislation.gov.uk/ukpga/2003/42/section/103A
- Sexual risk orders – sections 122A–122K of the Sexual Offences Act 2003: www.legislation.gov.uk/ukpga/2003/42/section/122

USE OF A POLICE PROTECTION ORDER

From the above list of protective factors, two would appear to be relevant to the case of the young girl. One option that the police have is consideration of placing the girl under a police protection order (PPO). This allows the police to immediately safeguard the girl under section 46 of the Children Act 1989 for up to 72 hours to prevent immediate risk of harm, which could be physical or sexual. Local authorities have similar powers under section 44 of the same act. For the police to enact a section 46 order, authority must be obtained from a police inspector. The police do have certain requirements placed on them upon using a PPO, such as informing the local authority where the child resides and informing anyone with parental responsibility of the PPO.

USE OF A CHILD ABDUCTION WARNING NOTICE

Another possible option would be to issue a child abduction warning notice (CAWN). In the circumstances outlined in relation to the young female and the older male a CAWN would be extremely useful, although it is not an enforceable notice but is an interruptive and protective measure. While CAWNs were originally intended for managing a child who went missing either through the action of a parent or a stranger, it has found a new application in relation to children entangled in CSE and CE.

DOMESTIC VIOLENCE PROTECTION NOTICES AND DOMESTIC VIOLENCE PROTECTION ORDERS

Another area where individuals can be extremely vulnerable and isolated is because of being the victim of domestic abuse. Earlier in the chapter the DASH risk assessment was considered as a risk assessment tool. One of the instances where it is extremely relevant is where an individual has alleged domestic abuse against their partner.

Domestic abuse is often described as a hidden crime and as such is under-reported (Barrow-Grint et al, 2022). This reinforces the fact that victims are frequently extremely vulnerable as a result of being a victim of this crime. It is important to understand, as far as is possible, the extent of the crime. In the year ending March 2021, there were 1,459,663 domestic abuse related incidents and crimes recorded by police in England and Wales. In this 12-month period 847,734 domestic abuse related crimes were recorded, representing a 6 per cent increase on the previous year and 18 per cent of all recorded crime by police in the same period (ONS, 2021). Table 6.3 identifies characteristics of domestic abuse victims which have been collated by the Office of National Statistics (ONS) in 2021.

Table 6.3 Characteristics of domestic abuse victims 2021 (adapted from ONS, 2021)

Victim characteristic	Comments
Gender of the victim	The victim was female in 73 per cent of domestic abuse related crimes in the year ending March 2021. This compared to 74 per cent in the previous year.
Age range of victims of domestic abuse related violence	In the year ending March 2021, the highest proportion of female victims of violence against the person offences, identified as domestic abuse related, were aged 30 to 34 years. Male victims were generally older, with the highest proportion of victims aged 75 years and over.
Gender of domestic homicide victims	Between March 2018 and March 2020, 76 per cent of victims of domestic homicide were female, and 14 per cent of victims of non-domestic homicide were female.
Age range of the victims of domestic homicide	Almost one in five victims of domestic homicide (18 per cent) were aged 70 years and over. By contrast, 1 in 20 victims of non-domestic homicide (5 per cent) were aged 70 years and over.

While the figures are based on statistics released by only 26 police forces, they do provide a useful view of the nature of the problem and provide some general indicators to assist police officers to consider the vulnerability of victims. While policing domestic abuse, particularly within intimate partner relationships, can be extremely difficult given the complexity of such relationships, the use of protective domestic violence protection notices (DVPNs) and domestic violence protection orders (DVPOs) can be useful as an intervention measure to protect the victim.

WHAT CAN A DVPN/DVPO ACHIEVE?

A DVPN can achieve short-term protection for a victim of domestic abuse. It can be issued after arrest, where a charge is not achievable or maybe where a perpetrator is to be released under investigation, or when no further action is available. It requires certain criteria to be in place.

- The perpetrator is over 18.
- Violence used or threatened towards the victim, or a person associated with the victim.
- The DVPN is necessary to protect either the victim or associated person from violence or the threat of violence from the perpetrator.

The DVPN initially authorised by a superintendent orders the perpetrator to leave the shared property for 48 hours as a safeguarding measure pending an application for a DVPO at the magistrates' court. A breach of the DVPN should result in the arrest of the perpetrator. If the court supports the application, the order can be granted for between 14–28 days. Breach of the DVPO is a civil breach of a court order.

The DVPN/O will involve partner agencies of the police engaged through the multi-agency risk assessment conferences (MARACs) and the engagement of independent domestic violence advocates (IDVAs).

REFLECTIVE PRACTICE 6.1

LEVEL 6

Reflect on the position of a victim of domestic abuse, the vulnerability of being involved in a close relationship, often isolated from any support networks through coercive controls.

- Do you think the use of the DASH risk assessment tool and mechanisms such as the DVPN/O provide sufficient protection to the victim?
- How impactive do you think partnership working will be through the MARAC group?

Sample answers are provided at the end of this book.

LIMITATION OF PROTECTIVE FACTORS

Having access to legislative protective factors such as DVPNs, DVPOs, CAWNs and PPOs and legislation which has been designed to address the types of offences being perpetrated against vulnerable victims is a considerable advancement on where policing was 20–30 years ago. The realist view, however, must be that sometimes the protective factors alone will be insufficient to deter determined criminal perpetrators who are frequently making fortunes from their acts of exploitation or gaining sexual gratification from their offending.

The simplicity of the offences which are perpetrated by offenders under CSE, CE, county lines, online bullying and modern slavery are often complicated when you add in the vulnerability factor. Chapter 3 considered factors both personal to the individual, but also those factors which caused vulnerability due to the situation and circumstances. The additional complications caused by the fact that sometimes an amalgamation of factors increases the risk to the individual, or the fact that an individual may only be vulnerable for a temporary period, adds to the difficulty for the attending police officer. Another aspect which adds to the complexity is the use of grooming and coercion by perpetrators. This makes a difficult task almost impossible at times.

THE COMPLEX CIRCUMSTANCES SURROUNDING VULNERABLE VICTIMS

Policing can now view vulnerability through a lens which defines the issues for all members of the police service and law enforcement agencies. So far, a great number of separate events where policing did not provide a satisfactory service to vulnerable victims have been discussed: Rotherham, Oxford, Operation Yewtree, domestic abuse victims and other more individualistic events involving single victims such as Victoria Climbié, Baby P and the case of Fiona Pilkington and her daughter. While there are a few factors that connect some of these cases, there are some golden threads of complexity which compound individual vulnerabilities.

One of main threads that can be seen in the cases of Rotherham, Oxford and many more CSE cases, modern slavery and county lines cases is the factor of grooming.

WHAT IS GROOMING?

Grooming is a phrase which is extremely prevalent in modern policing (College of Policing, 2021f). It is a term that is used to describe how a perpetrator builds a relationship with a child or vulnerable adult in order that they can manipulate, exploit or abuse the vulnerable individual. Groomers are often extremely competent manipulators, who not only befriend the victim but frequently their families too. Table 6.4 examines some of the common ploys used by groomers.

Table 6.4 What common tactics do groomers use?

Tactic	Comments
Online activity	On the internet groomers frequently pretend to be someone else. The murder of Breck Bednar is a case in point and will be examined shortly.
Authority figure	Occasionally the groomer will be a prominent person in the individual's life or have a position of authority which impresses the victim and their family. Jimmy Savile is an example here.
Generosity	Groomers will impress the victim by providing gifts, things that they want but cannot afford. This activity can last a long time as the groomer establishes a hold over the individual through gifts, often establishing a debt of bondage.
Pretend to be a child	This links into online grooming, as the case of Breck Bednar reveals. The pretence is to engage and entice the child victim and is a common ploy used by perpetrators of CSE.

CRITICAL THINKING ACTIVITY 6.3

LEVEL 4

Consider the common tactics used by groomers listed above in Table 6.4.

- Write a list of signs that a victim may be being groomed which may be witnessed by the victim's family and or the attending police officer.

Sample answers are provided at the end of this book.

Table 6.5 identifies some common signs that might be apparent if an individual is being groomed.

Table 6.5 Signs that an individual may be being groomed

Signs an individual is being groomed	Comments
Being secretive about who they are talking to online	This is linked to a change in behaviours and attitudes. Often related to online gaming.
Changing behaviour and attitude	Those with parental responsibility often note a change in both behaviours and attitudes. Individuals become demanding and combative, and change their current living circumstances, such as being online more or being online later.
Leaving friendship groups and appearing isolated	Individuals appear to leave existing friendship groups with whom they usually joined online gaming. This is linked to developing new friendships online.
Having new items which they struggle to explain ownership of	Quite often individuals will have new clothes, trainers, a new phone and it is clear they would not have been able to afford the items, and they are vague on how they obtained them.
Being online a lot more, particularly late at night	Linked to online activity and new friendships where there is a need to stay online much later than before.
Starting to use alcohol or drugs	An individual develops new habits such starting to consume alcohol and using drugs, influenced by their '*new*' friends.
Joining new friendship groups, often with older individuals	While the online world will introduce individuals to new people, individuals suddenly become very close to a particular individual who appears to be older than them.

EVIDENCE-BASED POLICING

The College of Policing considers the potential openness of defining the concept of grooming. Guidance can be found at www.college.police.uk/app/major-investigation-and-public-protection/investigating-child-abuse-and-safeguarding-children/police-response-investigating-child-abuse/risk-and-associated-investigations#grooming. It starts with the criminal offence which was created under section 15 of the Sexual Offences Act 2003 where any person aged 18 or older commits an offence if they have met or communicated with another person on more than one occasion with the intention of meeting that individual, travelling to meet that individual anywhere in the world, or that individual travelling to meet them, the individual is under 16 and they do not reasonably believe the individual to be over 16, and they intend to commit a relevant offence. (Relevant offences include those of a sexual nature.)

While the initial purpose of grooming is persuasive in a way that entices the individual into a friendship – providing that demonstration of support and encouragement which the perpetrator will emphasise only they can provide – they will attempt to alienate their victim from their support networks of family and friends. Groomers can be particularly confident and may try to in effect groom parents and guardians into accepting their presence with their children or other supported adults.

> *Grooming is the process of reducing the resistance of a child, their parents or carers to abuse. This may be achieved by increasing a child's, parent's or carer's fear of what might happen should they report the abuse and encouraging them to believe that the abuse is acceptable. Abusers often prime and control their victims.*
>
> (College of Policing, 2022a)

The initial sensitivity of the groomer quickly gets replaced by more sinister coercive behaviour by the perpetrator to maintain control over the victim once they have been enticed into the perpetrator's web. In Chapter 4, reasons why vulnerable victims do not report their victim status were identified. There is no doubt that the perpetrators establish an extremely strong bond with their victims initially and then entice the victim through psychological means to maintain the relationships. In many cases even an intervention by the police has not been sufficient to break the Stockholm syndrome which many vulnerable victims appear to be under the influence of.

POLICING SPOTLIGHT

THE MURDER OF BRECK BEDNAR

Breck was stabbed to death in February 2014 by Lewis Daynes. Breck was 14, while Daynes was 18 at the time of the murder. Breck met Daynes through an online gaming site where he knew some friends from his old school. Daynes claimed to be a 13-year-old boy but was noted to have an older male voice. Daynes made several claims about his life which Breck's mother became aware of, and she struggled with the veracity of some of the claims.

The essence of Breck's case is that he was groomed online by Daynes, who was both a determined manipulator and had acted in a similar way previously. Breck's mother became concerned, identifying the signs of change in Breck's behaviour and attitudes as he fell under the influence of Daynes. Such was her unease, she contacted Surrey Police to discuss her concerns for Breck. While she had suspicions and worries borne out of his changing behaviour, she was not fully aware of the dangers of online contact and the grave dangers of determined perpetrators.

→

Breck travelled to meet Daynes on 17 February 2014, having informed his mother he was going to meet his father. Within hours of that meeting Breck was murdered by Daynes. To compound the offence, Daynes sent photographs of Breck's body to Breck's younger siblings shortly after fatally attacking him. Out of the tragic death of Breck in February 2014 several positive outcomes were forthcoming.

- The College of Policing developed an overview of grooming to enhance understanding within policing.
- The importance of contact with the Child Exploitation and Online Protection (CEOP) Command was recognised as a support mechanism for concerned parties and an investigatory agency of what can be extremely complex cases (CEOP, 2022a).
- The creation of the Breck Foundation by Breck's mother Lorin LaFave. The purpose of the foundation was to ensure that no other family should suffer the same fate as Breck's.

> *Lorin travelled around the UK visiting schools, community groups, police departments, conferences and corporate companies to share Breck's story. Since 2014 Lorin has been dedicated to improving the digital resilience of everybody's children through the work of Breck Foundation.*
>
> (Breck Foundation, 2022)

For a fuller account of the case of Breck, consult www.breckfoundation.org

REFLECTIVE PRACTICE 6.2

LEVEL 4

As a police officer you are engaged in conversation with a parent who is expressing some concerns about their 14-year-old child. They have become quite introverted of late and secretive around use of their tablet which they use for online contact with friends. The child is refusing to discuss who they are contacting online or what they are discussing. The parent is unhappy but is unsure whether this is the child '*growing up*' and resisting parental control or something more sinister.

- Discuss how you would approach the conversation.
- What advice would you give the parent?

Sample answers are provided at the end of this book.

There are likely to be instances where children and young people are not being groomed online but are rather developing their individual character and starting to resist the constrictions placed upon them by parents and guardians. The prevalence, however, of online grooming which has been experienced through tragic cases such as Breck Bednar indicates the importance of concerned individuals being provided with the correct advice and support.

The professional curiosity which needs to be natural for each officer should lead to questions to determine whether an offence of grooming has taken place or may be taking place. But the professional police officer will now be aware of the support and information mechanisms in place. The Breck Foundation and the CEOP Command website are both online and easily accessible, with informative content and advice. Childline and the NSPCC sites also provide support and guidance in this area.

POLICING SPOTLIGHT

CHILD EXPLOITATION AND ONLINE PROTECTION (CEOP) COMMAND

The CEOP Command is now part of the National Crime Agency (NCA), having been absorbed as part of the national law enforcement agency in 2013 following the Crime and Courts Act 2013. CEOP works both nationally and internationally with a large portfolio of interest areas. Part of its portfolio is the targeting of online child offenders.

There are specialist police officers working within CEOP who track and prosecute sex offenders. CEOP works with a wide range of partners, including organisations such as the NSPCC, ChildNet, Barnardo's and companies such as Microsoft and AOL. They also work closely with many UK government departments such as those at Education, the Home Office and the Foreign and Commonwealth Office.

Take time to consult the CEOP website at www.ceop.police.uk/Safety-Centre/. It provides an extremely informative resource for police officers, partner agencies and concerned parents and guardians.

Advice for police officers who wish to contact CEOP or report an incident is that they should consult their force's CEOP single point of contact (SPOC) who will ensure that the intelligence or concern is passed onwards. The SPOC may be situated in the Force Intelligence Bureau or branch. Private sector reporting should be through contact with their local police.

One of the criticisms of Surrey Police was that their staff had not informed Breck's mother of CEOP and as such she was devoid of the advice and assistance which could have been provided to her and could have led to a different outcome. One of the pages on the CEOP site entitled '*Should I make a report to CEOP*' (CEOP, 2022b) provides advice to a child or young person, a concerned friend, a parent or other concerned adult. There are easily accessible links from this page to Childline and to further advice (CEOP, 2022c).

Once a report is made in relation to sexual abuse or grooming online to CEOP, it will be accessed by one of their child protection advisors. The advisor will contact the caller by phone or email address to ensure the individual is safe. They will discuss the next steps, but most importantly they will provide reassurance to the individual that they have not done anything wrong, and they will be helped.

One case study from the CEOP files relates to their first successful prosecution in 2006. A 21-year-old male called Lee Costi admitted grooming schoolgirls for sex and possession of indecent images of children. Costi was identified when a victim told her mother about Costi's chatroom messages and the mother reported him. Costi was sentenced to nine years' imprisonment.

SUMMARY OF KEY CONCEPTS

This chapter has considered how the challenges of vulnerability for policing provide a complex jigsaw puzzle to be resolved. Policing is faced with a multitude of enforced challenges in terms of crime types discussed so far, including online bullying and abuse, CSE, CE including county lines and modern slavery, but these investigations are further complicated by the involvement of vulnerable victims with their complex needs.

The key concepts considered were:

- the use of assessment tools; there is more than one assessment tool to assist the police unravel the complexity of vulnerable victims' involvement within crime;
- there are several protective factors which could be instigated before an offence occurs; these protective factors often have serious limitations and can fail to protect some victims;
- while lessons have clearly been learnt following tragic events involving vulnerable victims, the modern police officer needs to adopt a professional curiosity in order to both get the information to understand the issue at hand but also to improve their analysis of the individual circumstances of the vulnerable victims in order to safeguard them and prevent harm or the risk of harm.

CHECK YOUR KNOWLEDGE

1. What is the Vulnerability Assessment Framework?
2. What is a police protection order?
3. What is a domestic violence protection notice (DVPN)?
4. Name four signs an individual may be being groomed.
5. Name three websites you could direct a parent to who is concerned their child may be being groomed online?

Sample answers are provided at the end of this book.

FURTHER READING

Vulnerability-related risks: www.college.police.uk/guidance/vulnerability-related-risks
This guidance is strongly recommended for the reader to review in the context of improving both an understanding of vulnerability and improving the way police identify risks and safeguard individuals.

CHAPTER 7
THE POSITIONING OF A VULNERABLE INDIVIDUAL IN A WEB OF CRIME

LEARNING OBJECTIVES

AFTER READING THIS CHAPTER YOU WILL BE ABLE TO:

- critically consider the impact of intrinsic factors of vulnerability;
- critically consider the impact of extrinsic factors of vulnerability;
- evaluate whether individual perceptions of vulnerability exacerbate the problem;
- evaluate the support that is available to a vulnerable person.

INTRODUCTION

While it has been important to consider the types of offences which have targeted vulnerable individuals in recent times, it has also been pertinent to identify the factors both intrinsic and extrinsic which make the individual vulnerable to criminal perpetrators. It is axiomatic that certain offences mainly feature one type of victim. Child sexual exploitation (CSE), for example, when viewed through the lens of Rotherham, Rochdale and Oxford, identifies victims as being mainly young females. This allows an investigator certain commonality factors to consider when looking for trends. Other vulnerable individuals victimised by county lines gangs often lack such a common theme. Within the cases of Bijan Ebrahimi, Fiona Pilkington, Alice Ruggles and Breck Bednar there were intrinsic factors which in each case made them vulnerable to harm, but it is the additionality of extrinsic factors which considerably increased the risk of harm in each case.

This chapter considers the position of the vulnerable person in the web spun by the perpetrators in each case. It analyses the impact and influence of these intrinsic and extrinsic factors and examines why vulnerable individuals were failed, resulting in the most tragic circumstances.

AN ANALYSIS OF THE IMPACT OF INTRINSIC FACTORS

In Chapter 3, intrinsic factors were identified which could impact on an individual's vulnerability. These intrinsic or personal factors were noted to be individual and quite often these factors may only be temporary in terms of creating the possibility of vulnerability. It was also clear that quite often these factors had to be in correlation with extrinsic factors to create increased likelihood of vulnerability. Table 7.1 examines the intrinsic factors which can be identified from cases considered in this book so far.

What is interesting is that, except for Bijan Ebrahimi, the individuals who became vulnerable victims in the three other cases only really had one intrinsic factor, which certainly in the cases of Alice and Breck may not have rendered them as being vulnerable per se. This point illustrates both the difficulty for the police and their partners in identifying vulnerability as being a factor at certain points in an investigation, but also that quite often intrinsic factors alone would not always render an individual as vulnerable.

Table 7.1 Intrinsic factors identified in four cases

Case	Intrinsic factors identified	Comment
Bijan Ebrahimi	Ethnicity Learning disability Immigrant status* Language issue* Religion * There is a need to understand that these factors could, in certain circumstances, also be extrinsic factors.	Not identified as vulnerable. Repeat victim. Calls for service frequently ignored/ mishandled by police.
Fiona Pilkington's daughter Francesca	Learning disability	
Alice Ruggles	Gender	
Breck Bednar	Age	

Further critical analysis of the intrinsic factors in the cases of Bijan and Francesca also reveals the involvement of a protected characteristic – that of a learning disability. If Sophie Lancaster is also considered in this context, where the intrinsic factor of difference was identified, this does raise the possibility that hate is possibly involved in the targeting of some victims. The lessons learnt from all four cases identified similar themes:

- none were identified as being vulnerable;
- all contacted the police and had many of their calls either mishandled or ignored;
- all were clearly repeat victims.

CRITICAL THINKING ACTIVITY 7.1

LEVEL 4

Consider the case of Bijan Ebrahimi. Bijan was documented as having a disability, he was Iranian, an immigrant to the UK and he struggled to be understood.

- Analyse the impact of each of those factors in the context of when he complained about the abuse, damage and other offences that he faced.
- Write down how those factors may impact you as an investigating officer.

Sample answers are provided at the end of this book.

While each factor alone adds to the complication of the investigation, it is necessary to consider the impact of more than one factor at a time. The claim that the victim may be a nuisance or an attention seeker would be one borne out of an inability of the officer or staff member to gain a clear understanding of what the complaint is as a result of the intrinsic factors. Add anger and frustration of the victim to these factors and it is possible to imagine how some encounters end with negative rather than positive outcomes.

POLICING SPOTLIGHT

Police officers are expected to rigorously follow the Victims' Code when dealing with victims of crime. While in some of our cases crimes were not initially recorded by the police upon contact with the victim, those that were recorded are expected to receive a professional service.

The Victims' Code of Practice (VCOP), which was first created in the Domestic Violence, Crime and Victims Act 2004, sought to outline the entitlements of victims, such as all victims having equal access to the criminal justice system, regardless of age, location, status or offence committed against them. The most recent version of the VCOP was updated in 2021. (www.gov.uk/government/publications/the-code-of-practice-for-victims-of-crime)

The latest version of VCOP has 12 rights which police officers are expected to comply with. Table 7.2 below considers the minimum standards within the 12 rights.

Table 7.2 A summary of victims' rights (adapted from Ministry of Justice, 2021)

Victim right	Summary of right
To be able to understand and be understood	Understanding and clarification
To have details of the crime recorded without justifiable delay	Instantaneous reporting of crime
To be provided with information when reporting a crime	Provision with information to allow understanding of the whole process
To be referred to support services and have support tailored to your needs	Signposted to appropriate support
To be provided with information about compensation	Compensation details if relevant
To be provided with information about the investigation and prosecution	Provision of updates
To make a victim personal statement (VPS)	VPS explained and facilitated if wished

Table 7.2 (*continued*)

Victim right	Summary of right
To be given information about the trial and trial process	Date, location and time of trial and information relevant to the trial process
To be given information about the outcome of the case and any appeals	To be kept informed
To be paid expenses and have property returned	Payment of expenses and return of property
To be given information about offender post-conviction	Referral to Victim Contact Scheme where relevant
To make a complaint if the rights of the victim were not met	If dissatisfied with service – how to make a complaint

What VCOP 2021 shows is development of the understanding of the needs of victims of crime which needs to be understood in the context of the highlighted case studies. Table 7.3 analyses how the first four rights would have impacted on our four cases if they had happened after this most recent review of VCOP standards.

Table 7.3 Analysis of VCOP 2021 against the four cases

Victim right	Relevance to cases
To be able to understand and be understood	Bijan struggled to make himself understood. By adhering to this right, police would have been obliged to take the appropriate steps to ensure that communication was clear and two-way. Fiona, while not having issues communicating, was also unable to make the police and the local authority understand the gravity of the family's situation.
To have details of the crime recorded without justifiable delay	Crimes were not always recorded in the cases of Bijan, Breck or Fiona. Police are now expected to adhere to minimum standards for recording crimes and only in certain instances should an allegation of a crime not be taken seriously.
To be provided with information when reporting a crime	In the case of Alice, the choices provided to her around the issue of a police information notice (PIN) would suggest this was not made clear. While this right may be more of an overarching provision of information at the time of the crime report, proposed police actions need to be clearly explained in terms of likely effectiveness and impact.
To be referred to support services and have support tailored to your needs	It appears that in all four of our cases this did not happen, or certainly not with any degree of consistency. The provision of appropriate support is paramount and would have been necessary and required in all four cases.

AN ANALYSIS OF THE IMPACT OF EXTRINSIC FACTORS

Extrinsic factors were considered in Chapter 3, and Table 3.3 highlighted the main ones. Extrinsic factors were largely defined as being either situational or incidental. This includes the potential influence of factors such as adverse childhood experiences, adverse community environments, adverse cultural experiences, coercive and controlling behaviour, grooming, immigrant status, isolation, lack of power, lack of support, poverty, the presence of an abuser and using risky behaviour. There were some factors which the College of Policing determined to be extrinsic factors, such as language barriers and immigrant status, but these can also be seen as intrinsic factors in the case study of Bijan Ebrahimi.

CRITICAL THINKING ACTIVITY 7.2

LEVEL 5

- Consider the case studies of Bijan, Fiona, Alice and Breck and write down the extrinsic factors that are relevant to each case. Write a short explanation as to why they are relevant.

Sample answers are provided at the end of this book.

Which extrinsic factors did you consider to be pertinent to each case study? What reasons did you use to justify your thinking? There are some extrinsic factors, both situational and incidental, which have a bearing on all four cases. It is also clear that some extrinsic factors apply only to one or two of the cases. Table 7.4 provides an analysis of extrinsic factors that can be identified in the four cases.

Table 7.4 Extrinsic factors identifiable in the four case studies

Extrinsic factor	Identified in case	Analysis
Adverse community environment	• Bijan Ebrahimi • Fiona Pilkington	In the cases of Bijan and Fiona, they lived in situations where there was clearly community disruption and anti-social behaviour was a prominent reality to life.
Adverse cultural influence	• Bijan Ebrahimi	The Independent Office for Police Conduct (IOPC) report highlighted the likelihood that Bijan was targeted because of his difference around religion and ethnic status.

Table 7.4 *(continued)*

Extrinsic factor	Identified in case	Analysis
Coercive and controlling behaviour	• Alice Ruggles	Alice suffered from coercive and controlling behaviour, which subsequently moved into stalking and harassment. Breck was coerced and controlled online.
Grooming	• Alice Ruggles • Breck Bednar	Both Alice and Breck were clearly groomed by their murderers: Alice initially through social media and Breck via online contact.
Isolation	• All four cases	In all four cases, the victims found themselves isolated to a degree, linked to their lack of power and support that they received.
Lack of power	• All four cases	Again, in all four cases, the victims were powerless against the perpetrators in the circumstances that they found themselves in.
Lack of support	• All four cases	It could be argued there were elements of support in all four cases, but that it had no impact on the eventual outcomes.
The presence of an abuser	• All four cases	In all four cases, an abuser or abusers were present and closely engaged with the victim. Breck's case initially saw the abuser present through their online relationship rather than in person.

What the analysis does is recognise the impact of each of the extrinsic factors on the cases being studied. It also highlights the fact that some extrinsic factors could apply to most instances where a victim is identified as vulnerable. More importantly, it allows a professionally curious officer to understand both the relevance of extrinsic factors of vulnerability but also encourage them to look for signs that it may be the case.

THE IMPACT OF INTRINSIC AND EXTRINSIC FACTORS OF VULNERABILITY WHEN FOUND TOGETHER

In the four cases highlighted in this chapter, the identification of intrinsic and extrinsic factors has been considered separately up until now. In Chapter 3, a comparison was conducted in Table 3.4 in relation to the case of Alice Ruggles.

CRITICAL THINKING ACTIVITY 7.3

LEVEL 6

- Consider the combination of the intrinsic and extrinsic factors. Do you agree with the assessment of increased risk?
- Choose at least one of the remaining cases, Breck, Bijan or Fiona, and identify and write down which intrinsic and extrinsic factors are relevant to that case.
- Finally, write an analysis as to what intervention may have avoided the likelihood of negative outcome.

Sample answers are provided at the end of this book.

Which case did you examine? Which factors, intrinsic and extrinsic, could you determine? In the case you analysed, what intervention or protective factors did you consider could offset a negative outcome?

Table 7.5 provides a summary of the factors which made Bijan, Fiona and Breck vulnerable. When the intrinsic and extrinsic ones are taken together, they provide a clear picture, saying of Bijan '*this man is vulnerable*'. Do you agree? In hindsight, the sense of powerlessness and isolation of the family unit around Fiona Pilkington is evident. Only one intrinsic factor appears relevant, but it is exacerbated by a plethora of extrinsic ones. Finally, in the case of Breck Bednar; once again, one intrinsic factor is complicated by several extrinsic factors.

DO INDIVIDUAL PERCEPTIONS OF PROFESSIONALS EXACERBATE THE VULNERABILITY OF THE VICTIMS?

In the four cases, can a lack of empathy or sympathy towards an individual with an identifiable intrinsic factor of vulnerability be in any way considered part of the problem? It is a fair question. In each of the cases there is an element where the authorities did not respond to the issue of vulnerability in an appropriate manner.

Table 7.5 Intrinsic and extrinsic factors: Bijan Ebrahimi, Fiona Pilkington and Breck Bednar

	Bijan Ebrahimi	**Fiona Pilkington**	**Breck Bednar**
Intrinsic factors	• Ethnicity • Learning disability • Immigrant status • Language issue • Religion	• Learning disability	Age – 14 years old
Extrinsic factors	• Adverse cultural influence • Adverse community environment • Lack of support • Isolation • Lack of power • Presence of an abuser	• Adverse community environment • Lack of power • Isolation • Lack of support • Presence of an abuser	• Grooming • Lack of support • Isolation • Lack of power • Presence of an abuser
Increased risk	Bijan was vulnerable as a result of each of the factors listed. While separately some of the factors should not have made him vulnerable per se, when combined they meant that, without meaningful intervention and protection, he was more than likely to face a negative outcome at the hands of the perpetrator or perpetrators. The isolation and lack of support factors meant that Bijan was highly likely to be at risk from harm. An extremely vulnerable individual.	Fiona's family were vulnerable as a result of the factors listed above. While separately many of the factors would not have made her vulnerable per se, when combined they meant that, without meaningful intervention and protection, she was more than likely to face a negative outcome at the hands of the perpetrator or perpetrators.	Breck was vulnerable as a result of each of the factors listed above. While separately many of the factors did not make him vulnerable per se, when combined they meant that, without any meaningful intervention and protection, he was more than likely to face a negative outcome at the hands of the perpetrator. Breck's mother did attempt to intervene personally and through the involvement of the police, but this did not decrease or eliminate the risk.

→

Table 7.5 *(continued)*

	Bijan Ebrahimi	Fiona Pilkington	Breck Bednar
Intervention factors	• Taking Bijan to a place of safety away from the area where he was living • Obtaining a detailed evidential statement, free from misunderstanding and confusion over language • Taking positive action in relation to allegations which could be proved. Arrests of suspects, bail conditions, charges • Providing access to adequate support services	• Positive action around the allegations of anti-social behaviour • Ensuring full evidential accounts obtained • Provision of appropriate support for the whole family • Recognition of vulnerability of the family unit and acceptance that this was not a matter of minor anti-social behaviour or harassment	• Provision of appropriate advice and support at the point of first contact • Proper investigation and positive action • Recognition at the first call to the police should have instigated a police national computer (PNC) check on the perpetrator, the result of which should have been to ensure more positive action was taken, and the appropriate support and advice provided

BIJAN EBRAHIMI

In the case of Bijan, the police saw him as a nuisance and a serial complainer. It is clear from criminal and misconduct cases involving officers and police staff that some identified Bijan as a nuisance and did not empathise with him nor take his complaints seriously. Were the officers institutionally racist, as the Safer Bristol Partnership report (2017) stated, or did they fail in their professional duties? While it is easy to attach labels when failings have occurred, the individual professional failures are evident.

FIONA PILKINGTON

In the case involving the Pilkington family there is a similar apathy from some members of Leicestershire Police towards the family. The Independent Police Complaints Commission (IPCC) report made numerous recommendations around working practices, treating calls as individual matters, and not forming a bigger picture. The family lived in an area where the need for proactive patrolling was not considered and as such the actual situation that the family faced was not recognised nor was their vulnerability identified. Ineffectual measures were used on occasions, such as harassment warnings, which did not halt the abuse the family faced. Several officers were considered to have to answer for cases of misconduct. Rather than perhaps poor officer attitudes towards the Pilkington family, it appeared that there were training issues around performance that needed to be addressed.

ALICE RUGGLES

Alice Ruggles contacted the police when her coercive and controlling ex-partner caused her concerns. Police did act in relation to her calls, but the action proved too ineffectual and did not prevent the perpetrator from continuing his behaviour, until he eventually murdered Alice. As in the above instance, it could be considered that mistakes were not down to individual officer malaise, but more due to a lack of knowledge of stalking and harassment legislation, and a lack of proactive positive action.

BRECK BEDNAR

Similarly, in the case of Breck, a lack of training or understanding of the law based around grooming could be the issue and not the apathy of the officers to the report made by Breck's mother. It was also clear that this lack of clarity for call handlers around offences meant that no offer of appropriate support would have automatically followed.

IS THERE EVIDENCE OF INDIVIDUAL PERCEPTIONS BEING ANTAGONISTIC TOWARDS VULNERABILITY?

What the four cases have revealed is that, while the police have failed the individuals in all four instances, in three of them this is because of failings in their individual knowledge of the law, process or procedure, rather than officer apathy. In the case of Bijan, however, there is a clear picture that their antipathy towards Bijan meant that his isolation and lack of support when he needed it most was missing. This could be an indication that his actual vulnerability was not identified, and no adequate protection or safeguarding was ever considered. Wider consideration of other cases of child abuse, CSE and child exploitation (CE) through the lens of serious case reviews, inquiry reports and IOPC investigations identify some issues of individual officers and others lacking empathy for victims as well as the more generic failures due to knowledge of the law, procedures and policies.

WHAT SUPPORT IS AVAILABLE FOR A VULNERABLE INDIVIDUAL?

It has been established that vulnerable individuals can be victims of crime and targeted by those that would seek to exploit them. Their vulnerability is exposed by either intrinsic or extrinsic factors, or by a combination of both. The use of appropriate risk assessments to identify the risk of vulnerability and the prevention of the likelihood of harm have been discussed. The identification of harm or risk of harm then generates a need to protect or safeguard the individual appropriately. This can be established through a range of protective measures borne out of legislation or from the support of other agencies and organisations. Depending upon the complexity of the case and the vulnerability exposed, different responses to the vulnerable individuals may be required.

FORMS OF SUPPORT

Once vulnerability is identified there are several ways support can be obtained. Depending on the circumstances of the vulnerability, support can be determined at one of the multi-agency forums discussed in Chapter 4.

EVIDENCE-BASED POLICING

The multi-agency risk assessment conference (MARAC) arrangement was established to support and assist victims of domestic abuse. This is a very good example of where support for vulnerable victims can be identified. The College of Policing stated in 2021 that the safety of victims depended upon certain factors:

- an appropriate risk assessment and safety plan being created;
- a risk assessment which is a '*living*' document and continually reviewed throughout the case;
- a safety plan which is created to suit the needs of the individual;
- responsibility for keeping the victim informed is paramount, from the beginning of the investigation until the case concludes.

While the police are one agency at the MARAC, they can be joined by probation officers, health workers, child protection officers, housing officers, independent domestic violence advisors (IDVAs) and other representatives from both statutory and voluntary groups.

The provision of support for victims to gain advice, places of safety such as a refuge, the ability to be considered for special measures where the case is prosecuted and being kept up to date under the Victims' Code of Practice are again part of the wider picture of protection and safeguarding (College of Policing, 2021g).

SAFEGUARDING MEASURES

There will clearly not be a '*one size fits all*' response to safeguarding. Some vulnerable victims, particularly those of a young age, will need to be fully protected and removed to a place of safety, others might need advice to avoid sending money to scammers who target them while committing fraud offences. Individuals who are being abused online may need support and advice to eradicate the threat. Law enforcement agencies have a vast array of demands and requirements that they need to manage to both identify safeguarding needs but also to ensure they protect the individuals appropriately.

EVIDENCE-BASED POLICING

The National Crime Agency (NCA) documents how it has developed its responses to supporting victims and survivors. In Table 7.6 the various roles which have evolved to provide support to victims, particularly vulnerable ones, are considered alongside their activities.

Table 7.6 NCA supportive roles (adapted from NCA, 2022)

NCA support role	Activity
Witness care officer	To ensure the victim or witness is kept apprised of the investigation.
Victim identification team	To analyse images found in the possession of child sexual predators to identify, locate and protect victims of CSE and abuse.
Child protection team	To identify, locate and protect victims of CSE and abuse.
Specialist witness team	To provide specialist advice to manage vulnerable and intimidated witnesses and victims identified through all the NCA crime types such as modern slavery, CSE and abuse.
Protected person service	To provide protection where individuals are believed to be at high risk of serious harm – victims of honour-based violence, for example.
National vulnerable witness advisor	To attend serious crime incidents to advise on the development of investigative and witness management strategies where there are challenges with vulnerable or intimidated witnesses.

While the NCA has created these specific roles, within the national police services similar functions and roles will be undertaken by police officers.

VULNERABILITY AND COURT MEASURES

The ultimate aspiration of the police officer who has investigated a crime perpetrated against a vulnerable victim would be to have the perpetrator and offender charged to appear in court. In the past this has created several issues for vulnerable individuals who would struggle with the formality of the court system, which often would mean they were intimidated and unable to provide the best evidence that they could. In 1999 the Youth Justice and Criminal Evidence Act created a support mechanism called special measures. Follow the link: www.legislation.gov.uk/ukpga/1999/23/part/II/chapter/I/crossheading/special-measures

REFLECTIVE PRACTICE 7.1

LEVEL 4

In Chapter 6, a young girl aged 14 was found intoxicated in a public park with an older male aged 31. They were not related.

The male was arrested, questioned and following Crown Prosecution Service (CPS) advice charged with an offence in relation to the young female.

- Consider how daunting the courtroom could be for a young female victim. What do you think could enhance her evidence at the court?
- Write a list of recommendations which would help the girl to give her evidence to the court.

Samples answers are provided at the end of this book.

POLICING SPOTLIGHT

In terms of achieving the best possible evidence from a vulnerable individual, the investigating officer would follow the guidelines of the *Achieving Best Evidence* manual (Ministry of Justice, 2022). Once sufficient and valid evidence is obtained, the likelihood of a prosecution and a court case may follow. During the interview of the vulnerable victim or witness, certain processes would have been put in place to support the individual in that interview setting. The next stage for the vulnerable individual is to provide the evidence at court. Special measures were formulated following the 1999 Youth Justice and Criminal Evidence Act.

In essence, special measures can be recommended by the police and requested by the Crown Prosecution Service (CPS, 2021a) on behalf of a vulnerable or intimidated victim or witness where they believe that their vulnerability or intimidation will diminish their provision of their evidence. For special measures to be enacted, the court must agree to the request. There are several special measures that may be requested, dependent upon the specific circumstances of the case. Table 7.7 summarises the special measures which are available.

⟶

The pertinent sections which should be reviewed can be found in Sections 16 and 17 of the Act, which can be accessed through the links: www.legislation.gov.uk/ukpga/1999/23/section/16 www.legislation.gov.uk/ukpga/1999/23/section/17 and www.legislation.gov.uk/ukpga/1999/23/part/II/chapter/I/crossheading/special-measures

While the list of special measures suggests that policing and the courts can use such methods to protect vulnerable individuals, there is some concern that the police both do not identify cases where they could use them, and often do not request in cases where there appears to be a clear opportunity to do so.

> *... we know from previous research that the police have considerable difficulty in identifying vulnerable suspects and witnesses with learning disabilities.*
>
> (Burton et al, 2006, p 232)

Consider Reflective practice 7.1. Would you add to or change your suggestions to maximise the likelihood of the young girl giving evidence confidently at court?

Table 7.7 Special measures (Youth Justice and Criminal Evidence Act 1999) (adapted from Ministry of Justice, 2022)

Special measure	Comments
Giving evidence from behind a screen	Screening the witness from the accused so that the witness does not have to see or be seen by them (section 23).
Giving evidence by live link	The use of live TV link (section 24).
Giving evidence in private	Giving evidence in private (section 25) (limited to sexual offences, offences contrary to sections 1 and 2 of the Modern Slavery Act 2015 and offences involving intimidation).
Removing the formality of the courtroom	The removal of wigs and gowns (section 26).
Evidence provided through a video recording	The use of video recorded interviews as evidence-in-chief (section 27).
Cross-examined evidence on a video recording	Video-recorded cross-examination (section 28) available in all crown courts in England and Wales for section 16 Youth Justice and Criminal Evidence Act 'vulnerable' witnesses. Also commenced for adult complainants to sexual offences and offences contrary to section 1 or section 2, Modern Slavery Act, 2015 in certain Crown Courts.
Providing evidence using intermediaries	Communication through intermediaries (section 29).
Providing evidence using communication aids	The use of special communication aids (section 30).

SUMMARY OF KEY CONCEPTS

This chapter has considered several aspects which impact on the position of a vulnerable individual once snared in a web by a perpetrator. There is a reinforcement of the theme of complexity when considering the vulnerability of an individual. The content will assist you:

- to critically analyse intrinsic or personal factors as they impact upon the vulnerability of individuals;
- to critically analyse extrinsic or non-personal factors as they impact upon the vulnerability of individuals;
- evaluate whether the personal perceptions of professionals can exacerbate dealing with vulnerable victims;
- evaluate what support may be available to assist the vulnerable individual at various stages of the process of being a victim.

CHECK YOUR KNOWLEDGE

1. The Victims' Code of Practice 2021 (VCOP) has how many rights for victims?
2. What is the definition of an '*adverse community environment*'?
3. In the case study of Bijan Ebrahimi, what interventions may have changed the outcome of the matter?
4. According to the College of Policing there are four important factors which are required to safeguard victims. What are the four factors?
5. What legislation introduced special measures into the UK criminal justice system?

Sample answers are provided at the end of this book.

FURTHER READING

The revised Code of Practice for Victims of Crime provides an invaluable overview of the requirements of support for victims of crime. www.gov.uk/government/publications/the-code-of-practice-for-victims-of-crime/code-of-practice-for-victims-of-crime-in-england-and-wales-victims-code

Alice Ruggles Trust (2022) [online] Available at: https://alicerugglestrust.org (accessed 9 February 2023). The Alice Ruggles Trust was created to raise awareness of stalking. Its aspiration is to publicise the pertinent legislation so that it will be used effectively to both safeguard victims and prosecute offenders.

Safer Bristol Partnership Board (2017) *Multi-Agency Learning Review Following the Murder of Bijan Ebrahimi.* [online] Available at: www.bristol.gov.uk/files/documents/1225-multi-agency-learning-review-following-the-murder-of-bijan-ebrahimi/file (accessed 12 December 2022). The learning review into the murder of Bijan Ebrahimi provides additional information around the circumstances leading up to the murder and looks at all agencies involved.

CHAPTER 8
MEASURING PROGRESS: WHAT NEXT FOR POLICING VULNERABILITY ISSUES?

LEARNING OBJECTIVES

AFTER READING THIS CHAPTER YOU WILL BE ABLE TO:

- **evaluate how successful the police have been when dealing with victims with vulnerability;**
- **critically consider the areas where police responses can be improved.**

INTRODUCTION

This book has looked at the situation around vulnerability in the context of policing. It has examined how complex the identification of vulnerable victims can be; the imprecise science of considering the impact of intrinsic and extrinsic factors, whether alone or in conjunction with each other, has also been reviewed. It has considered theories of victimology and how certain factors such as adverse childhood experiences (ACEs) can increase the likelihood of both becoming a victim but also an offender. The context of why individual vulnerability was so important was determined through examination of key areas where vulnerable individuals were both targeted and victimised and by the realisation that policing had been responsive and, in many cases, had failed to identify and investigate allegations that could have reduced the victimisation of so many vulnerable individuals.

It is also clear that policing has been proactive along with other agencies and the government during the last 20 years in attempting to improve the way vulnerability was identified, how risk assessments were completed and ultimately how vulnerable individuals could be safeguarded. In terms of policing, www.justiceinspectorates.gov.uk/hmicfrs/wp-content/uploads/police-effectiveness-vulnerability-2015.pdf, the National Vulnerability Action Plan 2020–22 and the leadership of the College of Policing are united in the determination of a working and collaborative definition. The creation of multi-agency working groups focused on supporting vulnerable individuals and maximising communication channels between agencies is another positive step in recent times.

Chapter 7 examined certain cases involving vulnerable individuals and highlighted the importance of heeding the lessons of the past. This final chapter examines how successful policing approaches have been in the last 20 years, what '*best practice*' has emerged to provide a practical starting point for new police officers becoming engaged in the reporting and investigating of this complex area of policing, and where potential improvements can still be made. Finally, suggested recommendations are made for future development in this area.

HOW SUCCESSFUL HAVE POLICE INTERVENTIONS BEEN IN IDENTIFYING AND PROTECTING VULNERABLE VICTIMS?

REFLECTIVE PRACTICE 8.1

LEVEL 6

Consider the previous chapters and assess policing interventions in the last 20 years. Write down your thoughts in relation to the following questions.

- Between 2000–22, how would you view the overall success of policing in areas where vulnerable victims have been identified? Explain why.
- Highlight one case, explaining your reasons, where police interventions were particularly poor.
- Highlight one case, explaining your reasons, where police interventions were successful and created a positive outcome.

Sample answers are provided at the end of this book.

Consider your answers to the above.

- What thoughts have you identified?
- What judgement have you made in relation to the overall success of policing in this area?
- Which cases have you highlighted as examples of good or best practice and poor practice where a negative outcome resulted?

QUANTIFYING THE SUCCESS OR FAILURE OF POLICING INTERVENTIONS 2000–22

While it must be accepted that cases where failure has been identified, particularly those where tragedy has occurred, will attract media attention, cause public disquiet and often outrage, there will be many other cases where policing has been successful and protected vulnerable victims. These cases will not receive the same attention and certainly not the critical comment as failed cases would do. There are cases where meticulous police work has facilitated the achievement of positive outcomes for the individual(s) involved. This was recognised in the PEEL report in 2015 and is a key aspect of the College of Policing's '*What works*' site and in the development of evidence-based policing responses.

To attempt to quantify success or failure over the 20-year period under review, what actual assessment can be made in terms of policing interventions in the last 20 years?

POOR OUTCOMES FOR VULNERABLE VICTIMS

Table 8.1 examines six cases where policing has been considered to have failed the victims. Each case has been considered in earlier chapters, all of which can be seen to have certain factors in common.

Table 8.1 Poor or failed police responses

Year	Case	Main conclusions/recommendations
2000	Victoria Climbié	Inquiry – Lord Laming. His Majesty's Inspectorate of Constabulary and Fire & Rescue Services (HMICFRS) report. • Poor partnership working. • Poor police prioritising in terms of the investigation. • Poor supervision. • Inadequate training in child protection.
1997–2007	Fiona Pilkington	Independent Police Complaints Commission (IPCC) report. • Failure to recognise vulnerability. • Lack of consistency of supervision. • Incidents dealt with in isolation. • No recognition of repeated victimisation. • Lack of awareness of persons with learning disabilities were victims of hate crime (training).
1997–2013	Rotherham	Jay report. Independent Office for Police Conduct (IOPC) – Operation Linden report. • Inadequate training in child sexual exploitation. • Need to learn from the voice of survivors. • Poor compliance with Victims' Code of Practice. • Absence of strategic leadership, and poor supervision at investigation level. • Lack of use of protective orders.
2013	Bijan Ebrahimi	IPCC report. Multi-agency learning review. • Crimes not recorded in compliance with National Crime Recording Standards. • Failure to recognise vulnerability. • Failure to recognise repeat victimisation. • Recognition of unconscious bias.

Table 8.1 *(continued)*

Year	Case	Main conclusions/recommendations
2014	Breck Bednar	IPCC report. • Lack of training relating to grooming – call centre staff. • Failure to complete basic police national computer checks. • Failure to provide support guidance such as referral to Child Exploitation and Online Protection centre.
2016	Alice Ruggles	Domestic Homicide review (Gateshead Council, 2019). • Inconsistent approach to stalking. • Failure of public protection notices. • Poor use of police national computer checks. • Ineffectiveness of the Domestic Abuse, Stalking and Harassment risk assessment tool. • Ineffectiveness of training around stalking and harassment.

(*Note*: the IPCC became the IOPC in 2018, following changes instigated in the Policing and Crime Act 2017.)

From the six cases listed it is possible to identify common themes where policing has failed vulnerable individuals. These are highlighted below.

TRAINING NEEDS

One of the main factors which features constantly is the training of officers. Training where police officers are working with victims who are vulnerable is an area identified several times. Quite often failures have been identified where certain members of staff or police officers had not received appropriate training or had not understood the importance of that training. In some cases, such as Victoria Climbié and the child sexual exploitation offences in Rotherham, officers were poorly trained in dealing with such offences. In other cases, such as Breck Bednar and Alice Ruggles, there appeared to be an inadequate understanding of basic working practices around managing calls to the police for help. Quite often new or recent legislation appears to be problematic for officers and staff. This is evidenced in difficulties around implementing matters concerning stalking and harassment and hate crime relevant in many of the cases examined. This raises the question of why officers and staff may be inadequately *'trained'* or knowledgeable in *'new'* areas of legislation and resulting changes to policing practices. One simplistic observation relates to the implementation of self-directed online learning packages which became prominent in policing during the austerity period to reduce the number of officers on duty being called into classroom training, and the subsequent lack of engagement and understanding of the subject material. This is also often the argument considering the difference between training and education – the latter providing a greater level and depth of understanding and critical thinking.

SUPERVISION AND LEADERSHIP

Another common area where policing has been investigated for failing vulnerable victims is that of supervision and leadership. The importance of supervision cannot be overstated. Police officers investigate crimes or in certain instances may not record crimes. It is the role of the supervisor to oversee investigations and provide direction to the investigators to uphold the standards of investigation. Inquiries into the deaths of Victoria Climbié, Fiona Pilkington and her daughter and the child sexual exploitation in Rotherham all identified failings of supervision.

CRITICAL THINKING ACTIVITY 8.1

LEVEL 6

Consider the case of Bijan Ebrahimi. Reflect from the perspective of a supervisor.

- What scrutiny may you have given to the dealings of officers and staff with Bijan?
- What direction may you have given to address the vulnerabilities of Bijan and ensure that he received appropriate protection?

Sample answers are provided at the end of this book.

POLICE PROCEDURES

The theme of failing to adhere to recognised policing practices and procedures also links many of the cases. One factor in the cases of Breck Bednar and Alice Ruggles was the simple failure to complete basic checks on the police national computer. In both cases, such checks should have led to a different and more proactive response to the complaints which had been made. Some of the procedural measures that were not selected in certain cases also lay bare a possible issue of insufficient training or a lack of understanding. In the case of Breck, this related to both the provision of support and safeguarding measures as well as the arrest of the perpetrator. In the case of Alice, the initial interpretation of suitable safeguarding measures based around the distance between the residences of the perpetrator and the victim is relevant. The failure to consider arrest as an option when the stalking and harassment behaviour continued was pertinent.

PARTNERSHIP WORKING

The importance of partnership working is another common theme. The cases examined going back to 2000 have featured some examples of partnership working, although they mainly proved to be ineffective. In the earliest case featuring Victoria Climbié, police, social services and health services all had dealings and interactions with each other, but this partnership working did not protect Victoria. Quite often the lessons learnt in many cases such as Victoria, Fiona Pilkington, Bijan Ebrahimi and Rotherham have enabled positive developments to be created through multi-agency groups such as the multi-agency child exploitation forums (MACE) or multi-agency risk assessment conferences (MARAC) where greater collaboration between agencies is improving the safeguarding and protection of vulnerable individuals.

As a result of the inquiries and investigations into many cases, where the policing response to vulnerability was inadequate, improvements have been identified and, in some cases, changes recommended, resulting in improved working practices or new legislative approaches. It is right to reiterate that policing is not alone as an agency to have learnt from its failings and mistakes.

POSITIVE POLICING RESPONSES

The development of positive policing responses when dealing with the risk to vulnerable victims has been one of slow and steady improvement. Policing can be seen to have learnt lessons from the past and has been aided by a proactive stance from the College of Policing, supported by legislative changes, the advancement of multi-agency workings groups and the appropriate use of risk assessment models.

COLLEGE OF POLICING RESPONSE TO KEY DRIVERS FOR CHANGES TO DEALING WITH VULNERABLE INDIVIDUALS

In Chapter 2, key drivers were identified for change in the way that policing handled incidents involving vulnerable individuals. The PEEL report into police effectiveness around safeguarding in 2015, and the National Vulnerability Action Plan in 2020, both led to the College of Policing producing numerous positive actions in relation to improving the policing response.

- A definition of vulnerability for policing in 2021. This removed previous problems around inconsistencies when identifying cases of vulnerability. The lack of a consistent definition had also caused police officers in some cases not to recognise vulnerability in cases such as Fiona Pilkington and Bijan Ebrahimi.

- A focus on vulnerability and risk on the College of Policing website. This focus provided guidance for police officers in their approach to vulnerability and risk. The site can be viewed at www.college.police.uk/guidance/vulnerability-related-risks/introduction-vulnerability-related-risk

- The development of a policing approach or philosophy which demands officers to demonstrate a '*professional curiosity*'. This is one of the key pivotal mechanisms in the new approach demanded by the College of Policing.

- While the College of Policing has had a positive impact on the training of new officers through the curriculum developed under the Police Education Qualification Framework (PEQF), it also developed a bespoke one-day training course for all existing officers to enhance their understanding of vulnerability and to identify risk factors. The one-day course also emphasised the importance of professional curiosity of an officer when investigating circumstances which could involve the vulnerability of an individual.

LEGISLATIVE UPDATES

In Chapter 2 considered several new pieces of legislation. The Children Act 2004 was very much borne out of Lord Laming's report into the murder of Victoria Climbié and saw the creation of a children's commissioner and the local safeguarding children boards (LSCBs) in England and Wales. This is indicative of the government reacting to failings and attempting to provide legislative solutions. Another piece of protective legislation was the Safeguarding

Vulnerable Groups Act 2006. This legislation derived from the Bichard Inquiry Report (2004) into the Soham murders. Other new legislation was also highlighted which targeted certain offences where vulnerable victims are often found embroiled in the activities of the perpetrators, such as the Modern Slavery Act 2015, the Serious Crime Act 2015 and the Domestic Abuse Act 2021.

Proactive measures which could be used to support and protect vulnerable individuals were identified, such as a domestic violence protection notice (DVPN), a child abduction warning notice (CAWN) and the appropriate use of a police protection order (PPO). Each of the measures listed provides an opportunity, dependent upon the circumstances, to protect a vulnerable victim. In Chapter 5, Table 5.3 outlines the way certain measures such as a CAWN or a PPO could potentially disrupt a perpetrator and therefore protect the victim from the risk of harm and reduce their vulnerability.

CRITICAL THINKING ACTIVITY 8.2

LEVEL 6

An officer on patrol is approached by a concerned mother. The woman explains that her 23-year-old daughter has just started a relationship with an older male. She has heard the male had a reputation for violence against his last partner. The woman asks the officer if there is a way she can find out if the male has a violent past.

- What advice would you provide to the woman?

An officer answers the telephone in the parade room of the police station. A man asks for the officer's advice. His 9 year-old grandson has just started playing football for a local team. The grandfather is concerned about the coach's manner and language with the young boys. He asks if he can get the coach checked out.

- What advice would you give him?

Sample answers are provided at the end of this book.

In Critical thinking activity 8.2, the circumstances outlined provided opportunities in both instances for proactive measures to be taken, through applications under Clare's Law and Sarah's Law. These proactive or preventative measures are available because of failings in past cases, which have received legislative oversight to address areas where previous legislation was unable to assist.

PARTNERSHIP WORKING IMPROVEMENTS

In Chapter 4, partnership working was considered as one of the ways that the police and its partner agencies could work closer together to reduce the risk to vulnerable individuals. A variety of multi-agency groups were examined, including MACE, MAPPA (multi-agency public protection arrangements) and MARAC.

EVIDENCE-BASED POLICING

In Chapter 7, the purpose of MARAC was discussed. One of the key criteria for MARAC to be successful in protecting vulnerable individuals is by having all the key partners around the table. The key ingredient is information sharing. The College of Policing stated:

> *Senior officers should ensure their forces have well-developed and clear information sharing agreements (ISAs) with partner agencies. These ISAs should be regularly reviewed at force level and supervisors should monitor police information sharing to ensure that it complies with the ISA. Supervisors should, in particular, review requests from other agencies for information containing sensitive and personal details.*
>
> (College of Policing, 2018)

One of ten key principles of an effective MARAC was identified as information sharing. Information sharing should be relevant, proportionate and risk focused. Table 8.2 summarises the important aspects of information sharing between the police and its partners from principle 5 of the ten principles.

Table 8.2 Information sharing

What?	Why?	How?
All agencies attending the MARAC should prepare information for sharing.	At MARAC, all agencies should share the information. This allows risk to be analysed and solutions identified.	All agencies should be represented on MARAC.
All relevant and proportionate information and risks should be shared at the MARAC.	Analysis of all issues raised is required, leading to a personalised intervention plan which considers the risks to and needs of the victim.	All agencies should be confident to challenge the information provided where it increases risk or vulnerability.
All information should be distributed and stored securely.	Confidentiality is vital, and as such, risk should not be inadvertently increased.	MARAC information sharing protocols will be signed and adhered to by all agencies.

APPROPRIATE COMPLETION OF RISK ASSESSMENTS

A starting point for police officers is consideration of using the national decision model (NDM) (College of Policing, 2013a) when faced with a situation where decisions need to be made and justified. Risk assessment tools have been considered in Chapter 2 and further examined in Chapter 6 where it was determined that the appropriate use of a risk assessment tool was paramount in identifying vulnerability and the risk of harm that an individual may experience. Some risk assessment tools were specific to certain types of offences, such as the Domestic Abuse, Stalking and Harassment (DASH) model which focuses on victims of perpetrators of those specific offences. Others, such as the THRIVE model, were more generic as a risk assessment at the point of contact with the police to establish the appropriate response to the call for service.

One risk assessment tool appeared to be far more appropriate to policing when assessing the vulnerability of victims, and that was the Vulnerability Action Framework (VAF). It was recommended that the VAF be used alongside the NDM to provide a powerful risk assessment tool coupled with a decision-making structure which, driven by a professionally curious officer, would drive positive interpretations as to the status of the victim before them and highlight the areas where safeguarding is required. The simplicity of answering the questions around the following five areas provides a real opportunity to use the investigative mindset borne out of professional curiosity to establish the harm being experienced or the risk of harm if no action is taken:

- appearance and atmosphere;
- behaviour;
- communication;
- danger;
- environment.

HOW CAN POLICE RESPONSES BE IMPROVED STILL FURTHER?

The journey that policing has taken during the last 20 years has seen better working practices established and the creation of a national and corporate understanding of vulnerability within policing. That, however, is not and cannot be the end of the story.

Policing is constantly under scrutiny, both locally and nationally, and some of that scrutiny can often appear harsh and unfair. In terms of policing the areas of mental health, vulnerability and risk, much of the scrutiny must be accepted as fair and reasoned, and it has driven the changes in this vital area of policing practice to date.

WHAT CAN POLICING DO TO IMPROVE ITS SERVICE TO VULNERABLE VICTIMS?

Policing needs to police vulnerability consistently. Using best practice from around the country and learning the lessons from inquiries and serious case reviews, policing needs to ensure its response is both current, sufficient and appropriate. Ultimately, by evolving policing practices that are identified as having worked successfully elsewhere and delivering a consistent service to vulnerable victims, the overall service to those victims will improve.

But policing must continue to evolve even if performance in this area has improved, policing needs to be open to change and to develop its response to dealing with vulnerability. While policing has been quick to adapt to the criminal activities of modern slavery and county lines, and it has identified appropriate pathways for investigations and support and protection for vulnerable victims, it needs to be willing to adapt as crime trends continue to change. The recent publication of the Independent Inquiry into Child Sexual Abuse (IICSA, 2022) made recommendations as a result of offences of child sexual exploitation becoming a global problem and recognised the need to improve online safety. This is a clear indication that perpetrators will continue to adapt and use technological advances to their benefit. The police and other law enforcement agencies need to be flexible and willing to continue to develop and evolve in all areas to tackle the offence types that frequently target vulnerable individuals.

CREATING AN IMPROVED SERVICE FOR VULNERABLE VICTIMS

CRITICAL THINKING ACTIVITY 8.3

LEVEL 6

- Reflecting on the content of this book, particularly the challenges associated with dealing with vulnerable victims, write a list of three things that you will do in your personal practice to improve the service provided to vulnerable victims.

Sample answers are provided at the end of this book.

While the real responsibility for improving the service provided to vulnerable victims is organisational, there is much that an individual officer can do to enhance the experience of the vulnerable individual. They could:

- ensure that they take responsibility to obtain the most recent and up-to-date training for dealing with vulnerability within the requirements of maintaining their continuing professional development (CPD);
- ensure they are fully aware of support agencies that are available and be able to signpost victims to this support if appropriate;
- ensure they communicate effectively with the victim, listening carefully to what is said;
- ensure they use their professional curiosity to explore the situation before them;
- ensure they take personal responsibility for the investigation as appropriate in their role;
- ensure that all communication with partner agencies is clear and comprehensive.

While organisational responsibility to improve its service to vulnerable individuals is of prime importance, individual officers must accept the need to demonstrate individual responsibility and professionalism, or any organisational pledges will fail.

WHAT ARE THE MAIN LESSONS LEARNT?

The following recommendations will drive improvement in this area.

- The College of Policing and the National Police Chiefs' Council (NPCC) should ensure that any new legislation or new legislative practices are trained appropriately by police forces. While there are clearly issues over officer capacity and availability when implementing new legislation training, or training initiatives, consideration should be given as to whether self-initiated online learning is the best way to deliver new legislation and new practices to frontline officers. The lessons learnt would suggest it is not.
- The College of Policing should continue to collate and publicise best practice through its '*what works*' and '*evidence-based practice*' sites.

- Ensuring that police officers have sufficient knowledge and understanding around legislative protective and preventative measures and are competent in identifying and recommending the appropriate use of special measures.

- Listening to the voice of the victim and learning from their experiences.

- Ensuring that there is supervisory oversight of every case involving vulnerability.

POLICING SPOTLIGHT

There has been much attention in recent years on the role of the supervisor in policing. The College of Policing produced effective supervision guidelines to enhance the role of the supervisor. One of the guidelines, '*Acting as a role model*' (Guideline 4), is particularly pertinent in the context of policing vulnerability issues. In the cases of Bijan Ebrahimi and Fiona Pilkington issues were identified with regard to the lack of impact of supervision.

As a role model the supervisor must:

- consistently demonstrate high standards of professional behaviour. This would ensure that individual officers investigating issues around vulnerability had a positive role model to base their considerations on;

- encourage reflective thinking, an openness to personal feedback and a willingness to learn and develop, including a commitment to self-development. A supervisor who instilled these values and qualities in their officers would allow the development of professional curiosity in those members of staff;

- demonstrate an openness to new ideas and ways of working. This is important when using risk assessment tools which may suggest one thing, but professional curiosity indicates something else;

- challenge colleagues whose behaviour falls below the public's and the service's expectations. A key supervisory role is a prime way to ensure investigatory standards are upheld and that vulnerability is recognised and any necessary support identified and provided promptly.

More information on effective supervision can be found online (see College of Policing, 2022b).

This chapter has provided an overview of the way that policing has dealt with the issue of vulnerability in the context of crime. It can be viewed as a journey for policing in general, slowly appreciating the nuance of vulnerability, a nuance which far exceeds the simplistic interpretations of vulnerability that identified age and gender specifically. Vulnerability is identified through both intrinsic and extrinsic factors and can render an individual incredibly vulnerable to becoming a victim of crime. The difficulty, as noted earlier, is that this is not always a one size fits all labelling system, hence the complexity. There are many other vulnerability factors which have so far not really been explored, factors such as autism and other neurodiversity differences. The complexity of mental illness is another area where vulnerability can be easily exposed and is often a factor which is difficult to manage in the context of crime and victimology.

Policing, through the College of Policing and the NPCC, has demonstrated a willingness to evolve and learn lessons. There is a clear statement of intent to improve working practices within policing. The ultimate arbitration of whether this will be successful will be in the willingness and ability of every police officer to practice professional curiosity. If this is successful, then the developments and improvements of the past few years should continue to be made.

SUMMARY OF KEY CONCEPTS

This chapter has focused on several points around the summary of policing practice up to this point and looked at how the police and its officers can sustain and improve their approach to working with individuals identified as having vulnerability issues.

The content helps you to:

- reflect on how the police have dealt with victims with vulnerability through the last 20 years;
- use the understanding of policing practices over the last 20 years to consider how police responses can be further improved.

CHECK YOUR KNOWLEDGE

1. Which of the following measures would you inform the mother of a young girl who is worried about a coach driver who transports her 10-year-old daughter and teammates to gymnastic competitions to consider?

   A) Clare's Law or B) Sarah's Law?

2. The inquiry of Lord Laming into the murder of Victoria Climbié led to which legislation entering the statute books?

3. What does ABCDE stand for in the VAF assessment tool?

4. If a police officer requires guidance for dealing with vulnerability, which site should they be directed to go to?

5. What is the name of the most recent inquiry report into child sexual exploitation?

Sample answers are provided at the end of this book.

FURTHER READING

www.college.police.uk/guidance/vulnerability-related-risks/introduction-vulnerability-related-risk The link to the College of Policing guidance in relation to dealing with vulnerability is essential background reading for new police officers to understand the current ethos for policing in this area.

SAMPLE ANSWERS

CHAPTER 1

CRITICAL THINKING ACTIVITY 1.1

There is an extensive list of situations and circumstances where you as a police officer may come into contact with an individual who is vulnerable and at increased risk of harm.

Such individuals might include:

- an individual experiencing mental ill health, who is unable to make appropriate decisions to avoid being targeted by others;
- a spouse who is in a relationship where they are being domestically abused and unable to escape their situation;
- a child who is being sexually or physically abused by an adult.

CRITICAL THINKING ACTIVITY 1.2

1. Mental illness

2. Age, either elderly or young

3. Disability

4. The location of the individual

5. Under the influence of drink or drugs

REFLECTIVE PRACTICE 1.1

The use of the NDM is crucial to decision-making generally in policing, but more so in incidents involving decision-making around risk where vulnerabilities exist. The importance of adhering to the Code of Ethics is vital and will underpin a professional approach to THRIVE decision-making.

CHECK YOUR KNOWLEDGE

1. T – Threat, H – Harm, R – Risk, I – Investigation, V – Vulnerability, E – Engagement

2. Harm is either '*physical or mental damage*' or injury, and '*mischief or hurt*'. There is also the concept of social harm.

3. The main comparisons are:

   - situation and circumstances – personal factors, environmental factors;
   - unable to take care of self (or others);
   - likelihood of risk of harm (or exploitation, neglect).

4. The Victims' Code provides a series of minimum standards (rights) that a victim of crime can expect to receive from the '*relevant*' service providers.

5. Special measures could include:

   - screens (s23 YJCEA);
   - live link (s24 YJCEA);
   - evidence given in private (s25 YJCEA);
   - removal of wigs and gowns by judges and barristers (s26 YJCEA);
   - visual recorded interview (s27 YJCEA).
   - pre-trial visual recorded cross-examination or re-examination (s28 YJCEA);
   - examination of the witness through an intermediary (s29 YJCEA);
   - aids to communication (s30 YJCEA).

CHAPTER 2

CRITICAL THINKING ACTIVITY 2.1

- Baby P
- Victoria Climbié

- Daniel Pelka
- Fiona Pilkington
- Rochdale child sexual exploitation
- Rotherham child sexual exploitation

CRITICAL THINKING ACTIVITY 2.2

www.justiceinspectorates.gov.uk/hmicfrs/publications/police-effectiveness-vulnerability-2015/

REFLECTIVE PRACTICE 2.1

- Communication: speak to the alleged victim and build a rapport, communicate at an appropriate level, actively listen to their account, ask open questions, minimise personal biases, and remember the importance of non-verbal communication.

- Clues: payment in cash or card, any receipt, any CCTV at the house, details of tradesperson, description of tradesperson, any evidence of repairs being needed, paid in full? Any suggestion of shame or self-blame, fear of the offender.

- Curiosity: elderly victim living alone – network of family and friends? Capacity of the individual.

- Actions: 1 – Investigate crime, including house to house and CCTV reviews. 2 – Ensure intelligence submission is made. 3 – Arrange for reassurance patrols by neighbourhood policing teams. 4 – Proactively follow up any leads to arrest or deal with the offender. 5 – Ensure victim is kept up to date with the investigation progress.

CRITICAL THINKING ACTIVITY 2.3

See Table 2.6.

CHECK YOUR KNOWLEDGE

1. It was legislation to support an individual making their own decisions unless unable and to allow safeguards to be put into place.

2. Conducting a proper investigation, asking questions and keeping an open mind, not accepting everything at first value, testing your understanding, challenging your assumptions, being responsible – understanding the need to investigate and take action which is appropriate.

3. Answers could include:
   - definition of vulnerability;
   - use of risk assessments;
   - use of THRIVE;
   - investigations;
   - compliance with Victims' Code;
   - partnership working;
   - domestic abuse, missing and absent children;
   - preparedness to tackle CSE;
   - final conclusions.
4. That appropriate and consistent use be made of the National Police Chiefs' Council (NPCC) definition of a mental health-related incident (MHRI); the need to understand the cause of each incident in order to be able to identify specific mental health issues and to determine links to other vulnerabilities within the THRIVE approach; the need to evaluate any mental health indicators when dealing with victims, offenders or members of the public and signpost to the appropriate organisation or agency for support.
5. Sarah's Law – enables parents to enquire about individuals close by and whether they pose a risk to their child. Clare's Law – enables partners to enquire about partners and whether they have a previous history of violence against partners. Anyone can make an enquiry but only those closest should be provided with any relevant results.

CHAPTER 3

CRITICAL THINKING ACTIVITY 3.1

- Mental health issues
- Intellectual disability
- Physical disability

- Language difficulties
- Drug addiction
- Alcohol addiction

CRITICAL THINKING ACTIVITY 3.2

Three situations could include:

- a previous experience of ACEs;
- an adverse community experience such as poor housing or poverty;
- a violent perpetrator exerting coercive control over their partner in a domestic setting.

Three incidents could include:

- a young female being groomed by older male, presents, trips, praise, etc;
- a male in sheltered accommodation being pestered to let another man stay, seeks help from social worker but is ignored;
- an immigrant is victim of hate crimes, but due to language barriers struggles to convince the police of the problem.

There are many other examples you could have identified.

CRITICAL THINKING ACTIVITY 3.3

	Pilkington	**Ebrahimi**	**Common factors**
Intrinsic	1. Learning disability	1. Ethnicity	• Disability hate crimes
		2. Physical disability	• Not identified as vulnerable
		3. Religion	• Not identified as a repeat victim
Extrinsic	1. Adverse community environment	1. Adverse community environment	• Adverse community environments
	2. Isolation	2. Isolation	• Isolation
	3. Lack of support	3. Lack of support	• Lack of support
	4. Presence of abusers	4. Presence of abusers	• Presence of abusers
		5. Language barriers	
		6. Immigrant status	

CHECK YOUR KNOWLEDGE

1. Any five of the following – age, gender, difference, ethnicity, learning disability, physical disability, mental health issue, religion, sexual orientation.

2. Any five of the following – Adverse Childhood Experiences (ACEs), adverse community environments, adverse cultural influences, grooming, coercive control, immigration status, isolation, lack of power, lack of support, language barriers, poverty, presence of an abuser and risky behaviour.

3. Not following systems, practices, policies and protocols, inconsistent approaches to crime reporting, failure to report matters such as hate crimes, failure to identify him as a vulnerable victim and failure to identify him as a repeat victim.

4. 27 questions – how many can you remember?

5. Three levels, standard, medium and high.

CHAPTER 4

CRITICAL THINKING ACTIVITY 4.1

- Any of the protected characteristics (Equality Act 2010)
- Social status of the individual
- Security consciousness of the individual
- Lack of risk awareness
- Limited life experience
- Poor street skills

CRITICAL THINKING ACTIVITY 4.2

- Ensure incident is signposted
- Complete a Public Protection Notice (PPN). It has two purposes: for the police to notify partner agencies of a concern and as a risk assessment tool.
- Demonstrate empathy and understanding
- Gain trust

CHECK YOUR KNOWLEDGE

1. The correct answer in the circumstances is (iii)

2. Perpetrator – assertion of power – victim – child sexual abuse – powerlessness – perpetrator

3. Multi-agency child exploitation (MACE)

4. Professional curiosity – stop – observe – engage – report

CHAPTER 5

CRITICAL THINKING ACTIVITY 5.1

Child sexual exploitation (CSE) is a form of child sexual abuse. It occurs where an individual or group takes advantage of an imbalance of power to coerce, manipulate or deceive a child or young person under the age of 18 into sexual activity (a) in exchange for something the victim needs or wants, and/or (b) for the financial advantage or increased status of the perpetrator or facilitator. The victim may have been sexually exploited even if the sexual activity appears consensual. CSE cases include those in Rotherham and Rochdale. Individual predatory perpetrators such as Jimmy Savile, Stuart Hall, etc, are examples of offenders.

REFLECTIVE PRACTICE 5.1

The Jay report considers the victims' reasons, and the following are a selection of CSE factors which are evidenced by Jay.

- The child or young person goes missing regularly.
- A member of a dysfunctional or chaotic family.
- A history of domestic abuse within the family unit.
- A history of abuse against the child, including familial abuse.
- The child has social or learning difficulties.

- The child has low self-esteem or self-confidence.
- The child is excluded from mainstream education.

CRITICAL THINKING ACTIVITY 5.2

Answers may include (and are not exhaustive): the child being secretive, a change in temperament, a change in emotional well-being, peers and friends having older boy/girlfriends, involvement in petty crime, truanting, unexplained gifts and new possessions, change in appearance – new clothes, sudden drug or alcohol misuse, a sexually transmitted infection (STI), a pregnancy or seeking an abortion, and inappropriate sexualised behaviour.

REFLECTIVE PRACTICE 5.2

Answers may include:

- fear of the perpetrator;
- loyalty to the perpetrator;
- does not perceive they are a victim;
- believes they are consenting or acting voluntarily;
- holding a negative view of the authorities so less likely to report;
- fear of not being believed;
- shame and embarrassment;
- fear their sexuality will be questioned.

CRITICAL THINKING ACTIVITY 5.3

Answers may include:

- receiving threatening or embarrassing texts/emails;
- being sent or enticed to send sexual pictures (sexting);

- being sent offensive or upsetting images;
- being called names or having rumours spread about them on websites, forums or social media, being blocked from joining social networks or forums, or having their profile removed,to make them feel left out;
- someone creating a fake profile of them online and posting as them;
- being harassed and followed online, or someone online finding out their location and turning up there;
- may be someone they know or someone they do not, getting prank calls and non-stop texts, grooming activity – this is when someone encourages them to do things that they want them to do. They may pretend to be their friend, boyfriend or girlfriend but may not be who they say they are.

CRITICAL THINKING ACTIVITY 5.4

Answers may include:

- safeguard the individual – remove from any risk;
- if under 18 take to child-friendly, private location;
- obtain appropriate adult if under 18 or concerns regarding vulnerability factors,
- obtain an independent interpreter, not family member or peer,
- use the national decision model (NDM),
- consider modern slavery indicators such as evidence of a workplace being used for accommodation, workers who are distrustful of authorities, workers who look uneasy, unkempt or do not know work or home address, etc;
- inform line manager and liaise with specialist modern slavery investigator;
- check police national computer (PNC) and police national database (PND) and any local systems;
- investigate using achieving best evidence (ABE) guidelines.

CHECK YOUR KNOWLEDGE

1. *[A] person is vulnerable if, as a result of their situation or circumstances, they are unable to take care of or protect themselves or others from harm or exploitation.*

   (College of Policing, 2021a)

2. Answers could include: going missing for periods of time or regularly returning home late, appearing with unexplained gifts or possessions that can't be accounted for, experiencing health problems that may indicate a sexually transmitted disease, having mood swings and changes in temperament, using drugs and/or alcohol, displaying inappropriate sexualised behaviour, such as over-familiarity with strangers, dressing in a sexualised manner or sending sexualised images by mobile phone ('sexting'), increasing their screen time or showing unusual use of online platforms, such as websites, social media, apps or games, showing signs of unexplained physical harm, such as bruising and cigarette burns.

3. The National Referral Mechanism (NRM) is a framework used to identify and refer potential victims of modern slavery. The NRM is intended to ensure victims receive appropriate support. Statutory organisations such as the police and many non-statutory ones have a duty to refer obligation when identifying a potential victim of modern slavery.

4. Cuckooing is a practice where people take over a person's home and use the property to facilitate exploitation.

5. Section 1 a and b of the Modern Slavery Act 2015 states:

   A person commits an offence if –

   (a) the person holds another person in slavery or servitude and the circumstances are such that the person knows or ought to know that the other person is held in slavery or servitude, or

   (b) the person requires another person to perform forced or compulsory labour and the circumstances are such that the person knows or ought to know that the other person is being required to perform forced or compulsory labour.

CHAPTER 6

CRITICAL THINKING ACTIVITY 6.1

Table 6.2 provides an overview of suggested answers.

CRITICAL THINKING ACTIVITY 6.2

In the case of the young girl being found in the park with the older male, the risk assessment tools under consideration are assessed as being of use in the matter.

VAF – Yes, this tool is very useful for the officer to use in conjunction with the NDM.

DASH – No, in the circumstances provided this tool does not satisfy the situation faced.

THRIVE – Yes, although primarily intended as an initial assessment tool, it does provide a useful approach to the problem.

REFLECTIVE PRACTICE 6.1

The professional police officer, while wanting to use available protective factors on behalf of victims, will recognise that they have limitations in some cases. All intervention factors depend upon the will of the perpetrator to adhere to measures such as the domestic violence protection notice (DVPN), the child abduction warning notice (CAWN) or the police protection order (PPO) . What failure to adhere to the measures will more than likely achieve is sterner sentencing if found guilty at court.

CRITICAL THINKING ACTIVITY 6.3

- Being secretive about who they are talking to online
- A change in their attitudes or behaviour
- Leaving their previous friendship groups
- Possessing new items which they struggle to explain ownership of
- Being online a lot more, particularly late at night
- Starting to use alcohol and drugs
- Joining new friendship groups, often with older individuals.

REFLECTIVE PRACTICE 6.2

The first point is that the officer needs to be professionally curious around the details provided by the parent. Is an offence identifiable currently? If so, the officer should engage their investigative mindset.

If no offence is identified, or after recording details of a crime if appropriate, the officer should be providing support to the victim and their parents by referring to appropriate organisations and websites. Support such as the Child Exploitation and Online Protection (CEOP) site, the Breck Foundation, NSPCC or Childline, to name a few.

CHECK YOUR KNOWLEDGE

1. The VAF is an assessment tool which uses an ABCDE approach to gathering information: appearance and atmosphere, behaviour, communication, danger and environment.

2. A PPO allows the police to immediately safeguard a child under section 46 for up to 72 hours to prevent immediate risk of harm, which could be physical or sexual. Authority must be obtained from a police inspector. The police do have certain requirements placed upon them upon using a PPO, such as informing the local authority where the child resides and informing anyone with parental responsibility of the PPO.

3. A DVPN can achieve short-term protection for a victim of domestic abuse. It can be issued after arrest, where a charge is not achievable or maybe where a perpetrator is to be released under investigation, or when no further action is available. It requires certain criteria to be in place.

    - The perpetrator is over 18.
    - Violence is used or threatened towards the victim, or a person associated with the victim.
    - The DVPN is necessary to protect either the victim or associated person from violence or the threat of violence from the perpetrator.

4. Sudden secrecy about online activity, changes in behaviour and attitude, sudden departure from friendship groups, possessing new items but cannot explain how they came by them, increased online activity, particularly late at night, sudden use of alcohol or drugs influenced by others, and the acquisition of new and often older friends.

5. CEOP, Breck Foundation, Childline, NSPCC, Barnardo's.

CHAPTER 7

CRITICAL THINKING ACTIVITY 7.1

Disability – this should have caused a professionally curious officer to consider the possibility that the allegations made by Bijan were racially motivated.

Race – again, an officer should have considered the possibility the offences were racially (or religiously) motivated.

Immigration status – was this a factor which suggests an element of hate against Bijan?

Language issues – difficulty in communicating could be an issue, but it was necessary for the police to overcome this barrier to communication.

CRITICAL THINKING ACTIVITY 7.2

See Table 7.4 for suggested answers.

CRITICAL THINKING ACTIVITY 7.3

See Table 7.5 for suggested answers.

REFLECTIVE PRACTICE 7.1

The girl may benefit from one of the following special measures:

- giving evidence from behind a screen;
- giving evidence by live link;
- removing the formality of the courtroom;
- cross-examined evidence on a video recording.

CHECK YOUR KNOWLEDGE

1. 12.

2. A definition of an adverse community environment would include the following issues: a lack of opportunity, limited economic mobility, community violence, the effects of poverty and unemployment.

3. Some possible intervention factors could have included: taking Bijan to a place of safety away from the location where he was living; obtaining a detailed evidential statement, free from misunderstanding and confusion over language; taking positive action in relation to allegations which could be proved (arrests of suspects, bail conditions, charges and provide access to adequate support services).

4. Safety of victims depends upon:

   - an appropriate risk assessment and safety plan being created;
   - a risk assessment which is a '*living*' document and continually reviewed throughout the case;

- a safety plan which is created to suit the needs of the individual;
- responsibility for keeping the victim informed is paramount, from the beginning of the investigation until the case concludes.

5. Youth Justice and Criminal Evidence Act 1999.

CHAPTER 8

REFLECTIVE PRACTICE 8.1

Mixed views as to the success of policing in the period shown. Negative views may highlight CSE failings in Rotherham, etc, historic sex abuse scandals such as those investigated under Operation Yewtree, and others may consider the failings that led to the deaths of Victoria Climbié, Daniel Pelka, etc. Positive views may include policing responses to county lines modern slavery offences.

CRITICAL THINKING ACTIVITY 8.1

A supervisor would hopefully see the '*bigger picture*' in terms of the number and nature of calls made to the police by Bijan. This should have led to addressing the under-recording of crimes.

The failure to recognise the vulnerability of Bijan should have been easier to see by an overseer of all the investigations when piecing all the pieces of the jigsaw together.

The failure to recognise repeat victimisation, again, should have been evident to an intrusive supervisor.

Finally, a supervisor recognising shortcomings within investigations would have been more likely to recognise the potential of unconscious bias within investigating officers and attending staff.

CRITICAL THINKING ACTIVITY 8.2

The officer should advise the woman that she could make an application under the Domestic Violence Disclosure Scheme. This would allow the applicant to establish whether the partner has a previous history of violence or abuse. The police will complete relevant checks into the partner, and if a history of violence or abuse is established, they will consider if it is proportionate, lawful and necessary to make a disclosure. The disclosure would likely be to the woman's daughter in the circumstances.

The officer should advise the man that he could make an application under the Child Sex Offender Disclosure Scheme. This will require the police to research the coach to establish whether he has a record of child sexual offences. If the coach is found to have a criminal record for child sexual offences, then the police can decide to make a disclosure if they consider it proportionate, lawful and necessary. They would usually make the disclosure to the person ideally placed to protect the child, which in this instance may be the parents or guardians.

CRITICAL THINKING ACTIVITY 8.3

Any three of the following would be appropriate responses.

- Ensure that they have received the most recent and up-to-date training for dealing with vulnerability.
- Ensure they use their professional curiosity to explore the situation before them.
- Ensure they take personal responsibility for the investigation as appropriate in their role.
- Ensure they communicate effectively with the victim, listening carefully to what is said.
- Ensure they are fully aware of support agencies that are available and be able to signpost victims to this support if appropriate.
- Ensure that all communication with partner agencies is clear and comprehensive.

CHECK YOUR KNOWLEDGE

1. B.

2. Children Act 2004.

3. Appearance and atmosphere, behaviour, communication, danger, environment.

4. www.college.police.uk/guidance/vulnerability-related-risks/introduction-vulnerability-related-risk.

5. The report of the Independent Inquiry into Child Sexual Abuse (2022).

REFERENCES

Anti-Social Behaviour, Crime and Policing Act 2014. [online] Available at: www.legislation.gov.uk/ukpga/2014/12/part/9/crossheading/child-sexual-exploitation-at-hotels/enacted (accessed 15 February 2023).

Barrow-Grint, K, Sebire, J, Turton, J and Weir, R (2022) *Policing Domestic Abuse: Risk, Policy and Practice*. Oxford: Routledge.

Bartkowiak-Théron, I and Asquith, N (2012) *Policing Vulnerability*. Annandale, New South Wales: Federation Press.

Bates, C (2008) *MPS Response to the Death of Baby P*. [online] Available at: http://policeauthority.org/Metropolitan/committees/sop/2008/081204/12/index.html (accessed 9 February 2023).

BBC (2015) *Rotherham Child Abuse: A Year since the Jay Report*. [online] Available at: www.bbc.co.uk/news/uk-england-south-yorkshire-34002641 (accessed 9 February 2023).

Bichard Inquiry Report (2004). [online] Available at: https://dera.ioe.ac.uk/6394/1/report.pdf (accessed 9 February 2023).

Boddy, J, Statham, J, Warwick, I, Hollingworth, K and Spencer, G (2016) What Kind of Trouble? Meeting the Health Needs of 'Troubled Families' through Intensive Family Support. *Social Policy and Society*, 15(2): 275–88.

Breck Foundation (2022) *Helping Young People Reclaim the Internet*. [online] Available at: www.breckfoundation.org (accessed 9 February 2023).

British Association of Social Workers (2009) *Serious Case Review: Baby Peter*. [online] Available at: www.basw.co.uk/system/files/resources/basw_111257-10_0.pdf (accessed 9 February 2023).

Burton, M, Evans, R and Sanders, A (2006) Implementing Special Measures for Vulnerable and Intimidated Witnesses: The Problem of Identification. *Criminal Law Review*, 5: 229–40.

Care Act 2014, Section 42. [online] Available at: www.legislation.gov.uk/ukpga/2014/23/part/1/crossheading/safeguarding-adults-at-risk-of-abuse-or-neglect/enacted (accessed 9 February 2023).

CEOP (Child Exploitation and Online Protection) (2022a). [online] Available at: www.ceop.police.uk/Safety-Centre/ (accessed 9 February 2023).

CEOP (2022b) *Should I Make a Report to CEOP?* [online] Available at: www.ceop.police.uk/Safety-Centre/Should-I-make-a-report-to-CEOP-YP/ (accessed 9 February 2023).

CEOP (2022c) *Internet Relationships and You.* [online] Available at: www.thinkuknow.co.uk/11_18/ (accessed 9 February 2023).

Child Abduction Act 1984, Section 2. [online] Available at: www.legislation.gov.uk/ukpga/1984/37/contents (accessed 9 February 2023).

Children Act 1989, Section 17. [online] Available at: www.legislation.gov.uk/ukpga/1989/41/section/46 (accessed 9 February 2023).

Children Act 2004. [online] Available at: www.legislation.gov.uk/ukpga/2004/31/part/2 (accessed 9 February 2023).

Children's Commissioner (2017) *Defining Child Vulnerability: Definitions, Frameworks and Groups* Bright C. [online] Available at: www.basw.co.uk/system/files/resources/basw_83447-7_0.pdf (accessed 9 February 2023).

Children's Commissioner (2020) *We're All in This Together?* [online] Available at: www.childrenscommissioner.gov.uk/report/were-all-in-this-together/ (accessed 9 February 2023).

College of Policing (2013a) *National Decision Model.* [online] Available at: www.college.police.uk/app/national-decision-model/national-decision-model (accessed 9 February 2023).

College of Policing (2013b) *Risk.* [online] Available at: www.college.police.uk/app/risk/risk (accessed 9 February 2023).

College of Policing (2015) *First Response and the National Referral Mechanism.* [online] Available at: www.college.police.uk/app/major-investigation-and-public-protection/modern-slavery/first-response-and-national-referral-mechanism (accessed 9 February 2023).

College of Policing (2016a) *Mental Capacity.* [online] Available at: www.college.police.uk/app/mental-health/mental-capacity (accessed 9 February 2023).

College of Policing (2016b) *Risk-Led Policing of Domestic Abuse and DASH Risk Model.* [online] Available at: https://library.college.police.uk/docs/college-of-policing/Risk-led-policing-2-2016.pdf (accessed 7 January 2023).

College of Policing (2017) *Modern Slavery Definitions.* [online] Available at: www.college.police.uk/app/major-investigation-and-public-protection/modern-slavery/modern-slavery-definitions (accessed 9 February 2023).

College of Policing (2018) *Partnership Working and Multi-Agency Responses/Mechanisms.* [online] Available at: www.college.police.uk/app/major-investigation-and-public-protection/domestic-abuse/partnership-working-and-multi-agency-responsesmechanisms (accessed 9 February 2023).

College of Policing (2021a) *Introduction to Vulnerability-Related Risk.* [online] Available at: www.college.police.uk/guidance/vulnerability-related-risks/introduction-vulnerability-related-risk (accessed 9 February 2023).

College of Policing (2021b) *Curiosity 2021.* [online] Available at: www.college.police.uk/guidance/vulnerability-related-risks/curiosity (accessed 9 February 2023).

College of Policing (2021c) *Recognising and Responding to Vulnerability-Related Risks Guidelines.* [online] Available at: https://assets.college.police.uk/s3fs-public/2021-11/Recognising-responding-to-vulnerability-related-risks-summary-practitioner-evidence.pdf (accessed 9 February 2023).

College of Policing (2021d) *People and Places – How Resources Can Be Targeted.* [online] Available at: www.college.police.uk/research/what-works-policing-reduce-crime/people-and-places (accessed 9 February 2023).

College of Policing (2021e) *Evaluation of Think Family Early Intervention (TFEI) Key Findings and Implications for Practice.* [online] Available at: https://assets.college.police.uk/s3fs-public/2021-07/vvcp-evaluation-tfei-key-findings-practice-implications.pdf (accessed 9 February 2023).

College of Policing (2021f) *Risk Associated Investigations – Grooming.* [online] Available at: www.college.police.uk/app/major-investigation-and-public-protection/investigating-child-abuse-and-safeguarding-children/police-response-investigating-child-abuse/risk-and-associated-investigations#grooming (accessed 9 February 2023).

College of Policing (2021g) *Victim and Witness Care and Support*. [online] Available at: www.college.police.uk/app/major-investigation-and-public-protection/hate-crime/victim-and-witness-care-and-support (accessed 9 February 2023).

College of Policing (2022a) *Police Better Equipped to Spot Controlling Behaviour.* [online] Available at: www.college.police.uk/article/police-better-equipped-spot-controlling-behaviour#:~:text=The%20domestic%20abuse%20risk%20assessment,on%20coercive%20and%20controlling%20behaviour (accessed 8 January 2023).

College of Policing (2022b) *Effective Supervision*. [online] Available at: www.college.police.uk/guidance/effective-supervision (accessed 9 February 2023).

College of Policing (2022c) *Mental Vulnerability and Illness*. [online] Available at: www.college.police.uk/app/mental-health/mental-vulnerability-and-illness (accessed 15 February 2023).

College of Policing (2023) *Responding to Child Sexual Exploitation*. [online] Available at: www.college.police.uk/app/major-investigation-and-public-protection/responding-child-sexual-exploitation (accessed 15 February 2023).

College of Policing (nd) *Investigating Child Abuse and Safeguarding Children*. [online] Available at: www.college.police.uk/app/major-investigation-and-public-protection/investigating-child-abuse-and-safeguarding-children (accessed 9 February 2023).

CPS (Crown Prosecution Service) (2021a) *Special Measures*. [online] Available at: www.cps.gov.uk/legal-guidance/special-measures (accessed 9 February 2023).

CPS (2021b) *Rape and Sexual Offences*. [online] Available at: www.cps.gov.uk/legal-guidance/rape-and-sexual-offences-chapter-7-key-legislation-and-offences (accessed 30 November 2022).

Crime and Courts Act 2013. [online] Available at: www.legislation.gov.uk/ukpga/2013/22/contents/enacted (accessed 15 February 2023).

Cybersmile Foundation (2022) *Young Mother Commits Suicide Following Bullying and Abuse Online*. [online] Available at: www.cybersmile.org/news/young-mother-commits-suicide-following-bullying-and-abuse-online (accessed 9 February 2023).

DfE (Department for Education) (2017) *Child Sexual Exploitation*. [online] Available at: www.basw.co.uk/system/files/resources/basw_50313-9_0.pdf (accessed 9 February 2023).

Domestic Abuse Act 2021. [online] Available at: www.legislation.gov.uk/ukpga/2021/17/contents/enacted (accessed 15 February 2023).

Equality Act 2010. [online] Available at: www.legislation.gov.uk/ukpga/2010/15/contents (accessed 15 February 2023).

Every Child Protected Against Trafficking (2020) *Child Trafficking in the UK 2020: A Snapshot*. [online] Available at: www.ecpat.org.uk/Handlers/Download.ashx?IDMF=b92ea99a-6dd8-480c-9660-e6c0f0764acf (accessed 15 February).

Farrell, G (1992) Multiple Victimisation: Its Extent and Significance. *International Review of Victimology*, 2(2): 85–102.

Finkelhor, D, Turner, H A, Hamby, S L and Ormrod, R K (2011) Poly-victimization: Children's Exposure to Multiple Types of Violence, Crime, and Abuse. *OJJDP Juvenile Justice Bulletin*, 235504: 1–12. [online] Available at: www.ojp.gov/pdffiles1/ojjdp/235504.pdf (accessed 9 February 2023).

Ford, K, Kelly, S, Evans, J, Newbury, A, Meredith, Z and Roderick, J (2017) *Adverse Childhood Experiences: Breaking the Generational Cycle of Crime: Turning Understanding into Action: Summary Report*. Public Health Wales NHS Trust.

Fraud Act 2006, Section 24. [online] Available at: www.legislation.gov.uk/ukpga/2006/35/section/2 (accessed 9 February 2023).

Gateshead Council (2019) *Domestic Homicide Review into the Death of Alice Ruggles.* [online] Available at: www.gateshead.gov.uk/article/11258/Domestic-homicide-review-into-death-of-Alice-Ruggles (accessed 9 February 2023).

GOV.UK (2017) *A Typology of Modern Slavery Offences in the UK*. [online] Available at: www.gov.uk/government/publications/a-typology-of-modern-slavery-offences-in-the-uk (accessed 9 February 2023).

GOV.UK (2018) *National County Lines Coordination Centre to Crack Down on Drugs Gangs.* [online] Available at: www.gov.uk/government/news/national-county-lines-coordination-centre-to-crack-down-on-drug-gangs (accessed 9 February 2023).

GOV.UK (2021) *Victims of Crime.* [online] Available at: www.ethnicity-facts-figures.service.gov.uk/crime-justice-and-the-law/crime-and-reoffending/victims-of-crime/latest (accessed 9 February 2023).

GOV.UK (2022a) *Vulnerabilities: Applying All Our Health.* [online] Available at: www.gov.uk/government/publications/vulnerabilities-applying-all-our-health/vulnerabilities-applying-all-our-health (accessed 9 February 2023).

GOV.UK (2022b) *National Referral Mechanism Guidance.* [online] Available at: www.gov.uk/government/publications/human-trafficking-victims-referral-and-assessment-forms/guidance-on-the-national-referral-mechanism-for-potential-adult-victims-of-modern-slavery-england-and-wales (accessed 9 February 2023).

Henriques, R (2016) *An Independent Review of the Metropolitan Police Service's Handling of Non-Recent Sexual Offence Investigations.* [online] Available at: https://factuk.org/wp-content/uploads/2017/04/Report-Independent-Review-of-the-Metropolitan-Police-Services-handling-of-non-recent-sexual-offence-investigations-1-3-1.pdf (accessed 7 January 2023).

Henshaw, P (2021) *This is How Children Fall Through the Gaps.* [online] Available at: www.sec-ed.co.uk/news/this-is-how-children-fall-through-the-gaps-too-often-the-people-in-charge-simply-dont-see-them-anne-longfield-vulnerable-students-covid-19-pandemic-poverty-send-disadvantage-boris-johnson-education-social-care-welfare/ (accessed 9 February 2023).

HM Government (2018) *Home Office Serious and Organised Crime Strategy.* [online] Available at: https://assets.publishing.service.gov.uk/government/uploads/system/uploads/attachment_data/file/752850/SOC-2018-web.pdf (accessed 9 February 2023).

HMICFRS (His Majesty's Inspectorate of Constabulary and Fire & Rescue Services) (2015) *Increasingly Everyone's Business Report on the Police Response to Domestic Abuse.* [online] Available at: www.justiceinspectorates.gov.uk/hmicfrs/publications/increasingly-everyones-business-a-progress-report-on-the-police-response-to-domestic-abuse/ (accessed 9 February 2023).

HMICFRS (2020) *Both Sides of the Coin.* [online] Available at: www.justiceinspectorates.gov.uk/hmicfrs/wp-content/uploads/both-sides-of-the-coin-police-nca-response-vulnerable-people-county-lines-drug-offending.pdf (accessed 9 February 2023).

Home Office (2016) *A Typology of Modern Slavery Offences in the UK.* [online] Available at: www.antislaverycommissioner.co.uk/media/1190/a-typology-of-modern-slavery-offences.pdf (accessed 9 February 2023).

Home Office (2021) *Group-Based Child Sexual Exploitation Characteristics of Offending Group Based CSE Characteristics of Offending.* [online] Available at: www.gov.uk/government/publications/group-based-child-sexual-exploitation-characteristics-of-offending/group-based-child-sexual-exploitation-characteristics-of-offending-accessible-version (accessed 9 February 2023).

Homelessness Reduction Act 2017. [online] Available at: www.legislation.gov.uk/ukpga/2017/13/contents/enacted (accessed 15 February 2023).

Housing Act 1996, section 218A. [online] Available at: www.legislation.gov.uk/ukpga/1996/52/contents (accessed 9 February 2023).

Independent Inquiry into Child Sexual Abuse (2022) *The Report of the Independent Inquiry into Child Sexual Abuse.* [online] Available at: https://webarchive.nationalarchives.gov.uk/ukgwa/20221029013044/www.iicsa.org.uk/key-documents/31216/view/report-independent-inquiry-into-child-sexual-abuse-october-2022_0.pdf (accessed 9 February 2023).

IOPC (Independent Office for Police Conduct) (2018) *Learning the Lessons.* [online] Available at: www.policeconduct.gov.uk/sites/default/files/Documents/Learningthelessons/32/LearningtheLessons_Bulletin32_March2018.pdf (accessed 9 February 2023).

IOPC (2019) *Learning the Lessons – Mental Health.* [online] Available at: www.policeconduct.gov.uk/sites/default/files/Documents/Learningthelessons/34/LearningtheLessons_Issue34_February_2019.pdf (accessed 9 February 2023).

IPCC (2009) *IPCC Report into the Contact between Fiona Pilkington and Leicestershire Constabulary (2004–2007).* [online] Available at: www.report-it.org.uk/files/ipcc_report-fiona-pilkington-leicestershire.pdf (accessed 9 February 2023).

IPCC Final Report (2014) *Investigation into Police Contact and Response for Calls for Assistance by Mr Bijan Ebrahimi Prior to Thursday 11 July 2013.* [online] Available at: https://webarchive.nationalarchives.gov.uk/ukgwa/20180301152532/https:/www.ipcc.gov.uk/sites/default/files/Documents/investigation_commissioner_reports/Bijan%20Ebrahimi%20-%20Part%20B%20report%20-%20for%20publication.pdf (accessed 9 February 2023).

Jackson, J (2009) A Psychological Perspective on Vulnerability in the Fear of Crime. *Psychology, Crime and Law*, 15(4): 365–90.

Jay, A (2014) *The Independent Inquiry into Child Sexual Exploitation in Rotherham.* [online] Available at: www.rotherham.gov.uk/downloads/file/279/independent-inquiry-into-child-sexual-exploitation-in-rotherham (accessed 9 February 2023).

Jülich, S (2005) Stockholm Syndrome and Child Sexual Abuse. *Journal of Child Sexual Abuse*, 14(3): 107–29.

Justice Inspectorates (2020) *Both Sides of the Coin*. [online] Available at: www.justiceinspectorates.gov.uk/hmicfrs/wp-content/uploads/both-sides-of-the-coin-police-nca-response-vulnerable-people-county-lines-drug-offending.pdf (accessed 15 February 2023).

Killias, M and Clerici, C (2000) Different Measures of Vulnerability in their Relation to Different Dimensions of Fear of Crime. *The British Journal of Criminology*, 40(3): 437–50.

Loft, P, Foster, D and Kulakiewicz, A (2020) *Support for Children and Families during the Covid-19 Outbreak.* [online] Available at: https://dera.ioe.ac.uk/36613/1/CDP-2020-0106.pdf (accessed 14 January 2023).

Maguire, M, Morgan, R and Reiner R (eds) (2007) *The Oxford Handbook of Criminology*. Oxford: Oxford University Press.

Mental Capacity Act 2005. [online] Available at: www.legislation.gov.uk/ukpga/2005/9/part/1 (accessed 9 February 2023).

Mental Health Act 1983, section 136. [online] Available at: www.legislation.gov.uk/ukpga/1983/20/section/136 (accessed 9 February 2023).

MIND (2018) *At Risk, Yet Dismissed.* [online] Available at: www.mind.org.uk/media-a/4121/at-risk-yet-dismissed-report.pdf (accessed 9 February 2023).

Ministry of Justice (2020) *Codes of Practice for Victims of Crime in England and Wales.* [online] Available at: https://assets.publishing.service.gov.uk/government/uploads/system/uploads/attachment_data/file/974376/victims-code-2020.pdf (accessed 9 February 2023).

Ministry of Justice (2021) *Code of Practice for Victims of Crime in England and Wales*. [online] Available at: https://assets.publishing.service.gov.uk/government/uploads/system/uploads/attachment_data/file/974376/victims-code-2020.pdf (accessed 15 February 2023).

Ministry of Justice (2022) *Achieving Best Evidence in Criminal Proceedings – Guidance on Interviewing Victims and Witnesses and Guidance on Using Special Measures.* [online] Available at: https://assets.publishing.service.gov.uk/government/uploads/system/uploads/attachment_data/file/1051269/achieving-best-evidence-criminal-proceedings.pdf (accessed 9 February 2023).

Modern Slavery Act 2015, Section 1. [online] Available at: www.legislation.gov.uk/ukpga/2015/30/part/1/crossheading/offences/enacted (accessed 9 February 2023).

Namnyak, M, Tufton, N, Szekely, R, Toal, M, Worboys, S and Sampson, E (2008) 'Stockholm Syndrome': Psychiatric Diagnosis or Urban Myth? *Acta Psychiatrica Scandinavica*, 117(1): 4–11.

National Children's Bureau (2022). *Homepage*. [online] Available at: www.ncb.org.uk (accessed 9 February 2023).

NCA (National Crime Agency) (2018a) *County Lines.* [online] Available at: www.nationalcrimeagency.gov.uk/what-we-do/crime-threats/drug-trafficking/county-lines (accessed 9 February 2023).

NCA (2018b) *County Lines Drug Supply, Vulnerability and Harm.* [online] Available at: www.nationalcrimeagency.gov.uk/who-we-are/publications/257-county-lines-drug-supply-vulnerability-and-harm-2018/file (accessed 9 February 2023).

NCA (2019) *More than 1000 Children Protected in the First Year of Centre Tackling County Lines*. [online] Available at: https://nationalcrimeagency.gov.uk/news/more-than-1-000-children-protected-in-first-year-of-centre-tackling-county-lines (accessed 9 February 2023).

NCA (2022) *Operation Stovewood: Rotherham Child Sexual Abuse Investigation.* [online] Available at: https://nationalcrimeagency.gov.uk/what-we-do/crime-threats/operation-stovewood-rotherham-child-sexual-abuse-investigation (accessed 9 February 2023).

NHS England (2017) *Safeguarding Adults.* [online] Available at: www.england.nhs.uk/wp-content/uploads/2017/02/adult-pocket-guide.pdf (accessed 9 February 2023).

Newburn, T and Stanko, B (1994) When Men Are Victims: The Failure of Victimology. In Newburn, T and Stanko, B (eds) *Just Boys Doing Business* (pp 153–66), London: Routledge.

NPCC (National Police Chiefs' Council) (2016) *Policing Vision 2025.* [online] Available at: https://assets.college.police.uk/s3fs-public/policing_vision_2025.pdf (accessed 9 February 2023).

NPCC (2020) *National Vulnerability Action Plan (NVAP) 2020–22 (Revised).* [online] Available at: www.npcc.police.uk/Crime%20Ops%20Committee/NVAP.pdf (accessed 9 February 2023).

NPCC (nd) *What We Do and Why.* [online] Available at: www.npcc.police.uk/About/AboutNPCC.aspx#:~:text=What%20we%20do%20and%20why,the%20operational%20response%20across%20forces (accessed 9 February 2023).

NSPCC (2018) *Children Living in Families Facing Adversity: NSPCC Helplines Report.* [online] Available at: https://library.nspcc.org.uk//HeritageScripts/Hapi.dll/search2?searchterm0=C7167 (accessed 9 February 2023).

NSPCC (2020) *Child Sexual Offences Jump 57% in 5 Years.* [online] Available at: www.nspcc.org.uk/about-us/news-opinion/2020/child-sexual-offences-rise/ (accessed 9 February 2023).

NSPCC (nd) *What is Child Sexual Exploitation?* [online] Available at: www.nspcc.org.uk/what-is-child-abuse/types-of-abuse/child-sexual-exploitation/ (accessed 9 February 2023).

ONS (Office for National Statistics) (2020) *Religion and Crime in England and Wales February 2020.* [online] Available at: www.ons.gov.uk/peoplepopulationandcommunity/culturalidentity/religion/articles/religionandcrimeinenglandandwales/february2020 (accessed 9 February 2023).

ONS (2021) *Domestic Abuse Victim Characteristics.* [online] Available at: www.ons.gov.uk/peoplepopulationandcommunity/crimeandjustice/articles/domesticabusevictimcharacteristicsenglandandwales/yearendingmarch2021 (accessed 9 February 2023).

Operation Repeat (2022) *Operation Repeat.* [online] Available at: www.oprepeat.co.uk/ (accessed 9 February 2023).

Operation Yewtree (2011) *Operation Yewtree is a National Policing Operation.* [online] Available at: www.operationyewtree.com/about (accessed 9 February 2023).

Pemberton, S A (2016) *Harmful Societies*. [online] Available at: www.perlego.com/book/1657336/harmful-societies-understanding-social-harm-pdf (accessed 8 July 2022).

Plummer, M and Cossins, A (2018) The Cycle of Abuse: When Victims Become Offenders. *Trauma, Violence & Abuse*, 19(3): 286–304.

Police and Criminal Evidence Act 1984. [online] Available at: www.legislation.gov.uk/ukpga/1984/60 (accessed 15 February 2023).

Policing and Crime Act 2017. [online] Available at: www.legislation.gov.uk/ukpga/2017/3/part/2/enacted (accessed 15 February 2023).

The Protect Project (2021) *Child Sexual Exploitation (CSE): The UK Context*. [online] Available at: https://sites.gold.ac.uk/the-protect-project/child-sexual-exploitation-cse-the-uk-context (accessed 10 February 2023).

Public Health England (2020) *No Child Left Behind: A Public Health Informed Approach to Improving Outcomes for Vulnerable Children*. [online] Available at: https://assets.publishing.service.gov.uk/government/uploads/system/uploads/attachment_data/file/913764/Public_health_approach_to_vulnerability_in_childhood.pdf (accessed 9 February 2023).

Safeguarding Vulnerable Groups Act 2006. [online] Available at: www.legislation.gov.uk/ukpga/2006/47/contents (accessed 9 February 2023).

Safer Bristol Partnership (2017) Multi-agency Learning Review Following the Murder of Bijan Ebrahimi. [online] Available at: www.bristol.gov.uk/files/documents/1225-multi-agency-learning-review-following-the-murder-of-bijan-ebrahimi/file (accessed 12 December 2022).

SCR (Serious Case Review) (2009) *Baby Peter*. [online] Available at: www.basw.co.uk/system/files/resources/basw_111257-10_0.pdf (accessed 15 February 2023).

Serious Crime Acts 2015. [online] Available at: www.legislation.gov.uk/ukpga/2015/9/contents/enacted (accessed 15 February 2023).

Sexual Offences Act 2003. [online] Available at: www.legislation.gov.uk/ukpga/2003/42/contents (accessed 9 February 2023).

Stainton, I and Ewin, R (2022) *Criminal Investigation – The Professional Policing Curriculum in Practice*. St Albans: Critical Publishing.

Turner, E, Medina, J and Brown, G (2019) Dashing Hopes? The Predictive Accuracy of Domestic Abuse Risk Assessment by Police. *The British Journal of Criminology*, 59(5): 1013–34.

Victoria Climbié Report (2003) . [online] Available at: https://assets.publishing.service.gov.uk/government/uploads/system/uploads/attachment_data/file/273183/5730.pdf (accessed 14 January 2023).

VKPP (Vulnerability Knowledge and Practice Programme) (2023) *National Vulnerability Action Plan*. [online] Available at: www.vkpp.org.uk/assets/Files/NVAP-with-Interim-Measures-2023.pdf (accessed 15 February 2023).

Wright, K, and McGlen, I (2012) Mental Health Emergencies: Using a Structured Assessment Framework. *Nursing Standard*, 27(7): 48–56.

Young Minds (2018) *Understanding Trauma and Adversity*. [online] Available at: www.youngminds.org.uk/professional/resources/understanding-trauma-and-adversity/#:~:text=Adverse%20childhood%20experiences%20(ACEs)%20are,security%2C%20trust%20or%20bodily%20integrity (accessed 15 February 2023).

Youth Justice and Criminal Evidence Act (YJCEA) (1999). [online] Available at: www.legislation.gov.uk/ukpga/1999/23 (accessed 9 February 2023).

INDEX

Note: Page numbers in bold and italics denote tables and figures, respectively.